IVANKA TRUMP
AND
JARED KUSHNER

POWER COUPLES™

IVANKA TRUMP
AND
JARED KUSHNER

Adam Furgang

Rosen
YA™
New York

Published in 2020 by The Rosen Publishing Group, Inc.
29 East 21st Street, New York, NY 10010

Library of Congress Cataloging-in-Publication Data

Names: Furgang, Adam, author.
Title: Ivanka Trump and Jared Kushner / Adam Furgang.
Description: First edition. | New York: Rosen Publishing, 2020. | Series: Power couples
| Includes bibliographical references and index.
Identifiers: LCCN 2018048096 | ISBN 9781508188827 (library bound) | ISBN
9781508188810 (pbk.)
Subjects: LCSH: Trump, Donald, 1946– —Family. | Presidents—United States—Family.
| Trump, Ivanka, 1981– | Kushner, Jared, 1981– | Businesspeople—United States—
Biography. | Children of presidents—United States—Biography. | Presidents—United
States—Staff—Biography.
Classification: LCC E914 .F87 2020 | DDC 973.933092/2—dc23
LC record available at https://lccn.loc.gov/2018048096

Manufactured in China

On the cover: On April 24, 2018, Ivanka Trump and Jared Kushner attend a state
dinner at the White House in honor of President Emmanuel Macron of France.

CONTENTS

INTRODUCTION 6

CHAPTER 1
IVANKA: FROM THE START 9

CHAPTER 2
JARED: THE ORIGIN STORY 21

CHAPTER 3
MEETING OF THE MINDS 33

CHAPTER 4
THE YIN AND YANG OF TRUMP AND KUSHNER 43

CHAPTER 5
YOU'RE HIRED! DONALD TRUMP WINS PRESIDENCY 56

CHAPTER 6
ADVISERS TO THE PRESIDENT 65

CHAPTER 7
FROM THE BIG APPLE TO DC 76

TIMELINE 88

GLOSSARY 90

FOR MORE INFORMATION 92

FOR FURTHER READING 94

BIBLIOGRAPHY 95

INDEX 108

INTRODUCTION

There are power couples and then there are those couples who are powerful on a whole other level. Ivanka Trump and Jared Kushner met in 2007, married in 2009, and quickly became one of the world's most powerful power couples in the sphere of government.

The first half of the power couple of Ivanka Trump and Jared Kushner (sometimes playfully referred to in the media as "Javanka") is Ivanka Trump. Trump is the eldest daughter of the forty-fifth president of the United States, Donald J. Trump. Her mother, Ivana Trump, is a former fashion model. Ivanka grew up with wealth and privilege in her father's famous skyscraper building, Trump Tower, in New York City. She has worked as a fashion model, written several books about the business world, and served as an executive vice president for the Trump Organization. She was also the chief executive officer (CEO) of her own fashion company, the Ivanka Trump lifestyle brand.

The other half of the "Javanka" power couple is Jared Kushner. Kushner is the eldest son of billionaire real estate developer Charles Kushner. Like Ivanka, Kushner grew up surrounded by wealth and privilege. He attended Harvard University and majored in government. At age twenty-five, before he had even finished graduate school at New York

Jared Kushner and Ivanka Trump attend a benefit at the Metropolitan Museum of Art in New York City in 2014.

University, Kushner became the owner of the *New York Observer*, a weekly newspaper.

Ivanka and Jared met at a business lunch arranged by one of Ivanka's colleagues. They dated for several years and eventually married. Their work, separately and as a couple, allowed them to become one of the most influential power couples in the world. They helped Donald Trump win the 2016 US presidential election, and then they served as advisers in the Trump presidency. Their businesses and investments continued as well. Ivanka Trump and Jared Kushner together earned at least $81 million in 2017, according to a June 2018 report in *USA Today*.

Trump and Kushner are not the first married couple to be labeled as a "power couple." The *Oxford English Dictionary* defines a power couple as "a couple consisting of two people who are each influential or successful in their own right."

One of the first uses of the term "power couple" began in 1983 to describe US Republican senators Bob and Elizabeth Dole—both of whom went on to run for president of the United States. The term then became popular in the mid 1980s. Since then, it has been used to describe not only political couples but also media celebrities such as Beyoncé and Jay-Z and Kim Kardashian West and Kanye West. According to a Huffington Post article by Maddie Crum from 2016, the *Oxford English Dictionary* added the term "power couple" to its entries in June of that year. Since they married in 2009, Ivanka Trump and Jared Kushner have lived up to the definition of the term.

CHAPTER 1

IVANKA: FROM THE START

As a businessman, a real estate tycoon, reality television star, and today as the president of the United States, Donald J. Trump has dominated media and tabloid headlines for decades. He has also been married three times and has five children. His firstborn daughter, Ivanka Trump, grew up following closely in her father's footsteps. Once she became an adult, however, she quickly stepped out on her own and made a name for herself as a fashion model, author, film and TV personality, real estate developer, and the creator of her own fashion and jewelry company, the Ivanka Trump collection. She accomplished all of these feats before becoming an unpaid adviser in the White House to her father when he became president of the United States.

IVANKA'S FATHER: DONALD TRUMP

Ivanka Trump's father, Donald J. Trump, was born in Queens, New York, on June 14, 1946. His parents, Frederick and Mary Anne Trump, both came from European ancestry. Frederick Trump, called Fred, was the son of German immigrants, and Mary Anne Trump (born Mary MacLeod) emigrated from Tong, Scotland, in 1929 when she was seventeen years old. Fred and Mary married in 1936 and lived in the Jamaica Estates section of Queens, a borough of New York City, and had five children. After World War II (1939–1945), real estate developer Fred Trump became wealthy constructing apartments in the New York City boroughs of Queens and Staten Island.

While growing up, Donald Trump attended the private Kew Forest School in Forest Hills, Queens. When he was thirteen, he enrolled in the New York Military Academy, where he continued his studies until college. He went on to study at Fordham University in the Bronx for two years and then transferred to the University of Pennsylvania to study economics. He graduated from that school in 1968. Trump also attended undergraduate classes at the renowned Wharton School of Business, where his daughter, Ivanka, would eventually graduate.

IVANKA'S MOTHER: IVANA TRUMP

Here, Donald J. Trump is pictured with his father, Fred. The Trumps are longtime residents and real estate developers in New York City. The Trump Organization repaired the famous ice skating rink in Central Park in 1986.

Ivanka Trump's mother, Ivana Marie Zelníčková, was born on February 20, 1949, in Gottwaldov, Czechoslovakia, which is now the Czech Republic town of Zlín. Zelníčková's father, Milos, taught her to ski and swim when she was only two years old. By age six, she was skiing competitively. At age twelve, Zelníčková enrolled in a national training program for skiers and soon began competing in European tournaments. In 1967, she enrolled in

After marrying Donald Trump on April 7, 1977, Ivana Trump gave up her career as a model and began working for the Trump Organization as vice president of interior design.

college at Charles University in Prague, Czechoslovakia, and graduated with a master's degree in physical education.

In 1971, Zelníčková married an Austrian skier, Alfred Winklmayr, and was then able to leave her communist-controlled country. She soon immigrated to Canada, learned how to speak English, and became a ski instructor. She then moved to Toronto, Ontario, where she started a career as a model in the 1970s. Modeling led her to New York City, where she met her future husband, Donald J. Trump.

GROWING UP IN TRUMP TOWER

Ivanka Trump's parents met in New York City in the summer of 1976 and were married less than a year later, on April 7, 1977. On December 31, 1977— New Year's Eve—Ivana gave birth to the Trumps' first child, Donald John Trump Jr.

Ivanka was born in New York City on October 30, 1981. She was named after her mother and given the full name Ivana Marie Trump. In Czech, her mother's native language, Ivanka is the nickname for Ivana. So, her parents began calling her Ivanka, and the name stuck into adulthood.

On January 6, 1984, Ivanka's brother Eric Frederick Trump was born. Just a few months later, the Trump family moved into a spacious apartment in an acclaimed skyscraper built by the Trump Organization, called Trump Tower, on Fifth Avenue. Ivanka was two years old at the time.

STARTING THE TRUMP ORGANIZATION

The Trump family real estate business began in the early 1900s after Elizabeth Christ Trump emigrated from Germany to the United States. When Trump's husband died, she was left to handle the real estate that he owned. She had houses built on the empty properties that her husband left her. She then sold the houses and lived off the money paid by the new owners. She wanted her children to take over the real estate business when they grew up. When her middle son, Fred—Donald Trump's father—wanted

(continued on the next page)

"

(continued from the previous page)

Rather than getting Barbie dolls ... I always wanted Legos or Erector sets ... I love looking at the New York skyline and being able to figure out what I'm going to add to that ... I've always wanted to go into real-estate development."

—IVANKA TRUMP

to take over the business early, she started a company and called it Elizabeth Trump & Son. From there, Fred made the family business even more successful and founded what is now known as the Trump Organization. The real estate business made the Trump family members the rich and famous individuals whom people know today.

In the 2003 documentary *Born Rich*, a young Ivanka Trump was interviewed about her plans in real estate development. Her ideas mirrored her great-grandmother's. She stated, "Rather than getting Barbie dolls—I used to get upset—I always wanted Legos or Erector sets." Trump said in the film, "I love looking at the New York skyline and being able to figure out what I'm going to add to that and what patch of sky one of my buildings will be in. I've always wanted to go into real-estate development."

The three Trump children, along with two nannies, had an entire floor at the top of the three-story penthouse all to themselves, the sixty-eighth floor of Trump Tower. The penthouse had amazing views of

Ivanka (*right*) and her brother Eric (*left*), grew up in Trump Tower. They attended many charity events, and in 1993, they participated in the United States Marine Corps Toys for Tots Benefit Gala.

Manhattan. The children's floor had a room for each child, a room for the nannies to share, two guest rooms, and a kitchen. The family penthouse even had its own elevator.

Ivanka's bedroom had posters of the pop music singer Madonna as well as pictures from the popular TV show at the time, *Beverly Hills 90210*. Her bedroom also had floor-to-ceiling windows with a full view of Central Park.

Another room dedicated to the three Trump children was a playroom, which had toys, video games, videotapes, and a big-screen TV. Meeting celebrities was common for the Trump children. One of the famous neighbors in the building and a good friend to the Trump family was pop star Michael Jackson, who would often visit to play video games with the Trump children. According

While she was modeling as a teen, Ivanka accompanied her mother, Ivana, to many fashion events. In April 1995, they took part in Fashion Week Fashions by Ralph Lauren.

to Ivanka's mother, in her book *Raising Trump*, "the only person who had an open invitation to come to the triplex for playdates whenever he wanted was Michael Jackson … He'd stop by and chat with Donald and me for twenty minutes, and then he'd go up to the kids' floor to hang out with them for hours and hours," she said. "They'd watch MTV, play Mario Brothers or Tetris, and build Trump Tower in Legos."

Growing up, Ivanka gravitated toward the arts, and she studied ballet and piano for several years. Michael Jackson also visited Ivanka at a Christmas performance of *The Nutcracker* that the New York City Ballet performed at Lincoln Center.

For her grade school years, Ivanka went to the all-girls private Chapin School in Manhattan, which

THE EXTENDED TRUMP FAMILY

When parents get divorced it is never easy for children, but when your parents are famous and it's in the news every day, the unraveling of a marriage can be especially rough. Ivanka's parents split up when she was eight, and their divorce was finalized in 1992, when she was just ten. The story received constant attention in the media during that time, which was difficult for the Trump children.

Donald Trump married Marla Maples on December 20, 1993, less than a year after his divorce from Ivana Trump. They had one child, Tiffany Ariana, who was born on October 13, 1993, in West Palm Beach, Florida. Trump and Maples divorced in 1999.

Trump then married Melania Knauss on January 22, 2005. They have one child, Barron William, who was born on March 20, 2006, in New York City. Barron is the only one of the five Trump children who has lived in the White House with his father.

Jackie Bouvier Kennedy had once attended. At age fifteen, she transferred to a boarding school, Choate Rosemary Hall in Wallingford, Connecticut, where John F. Kennedy had once attended. Esteemed architect I. M. Pei designed both the Icahn Center for Science and the Paul Mellon Arts Center at Choate Rosemary Hall School.

Ivanka was not entirely happy being away at boarding school. According to a 2007 *Marie Claire* article by George Gurley, Ivanka said, "I was all of a sudden in the prison of boarding-school life, and all my friends in New York were having fun."

After graduating from Choate Rosemary Hall in June 2000, Ivanka went to college at Georgetown University for two years before transferring to the Wharton School at the University of Pennsylvania. She went on to graduate summa cum laude, a Latin phrase that means "with greatest honor." She received a bachelor of science degree in economics from the Wharton School when she graduated in 2004.

ON HER OWN

As Ivanka grew up, she would sometimes accompany her mother to the fashion shows of elite designers in Paris, France. In her teens, Ivanka gravitated naturally toward her mother's career, modeling. According to her mother, Ivanka modeled when it would not interfere with her schoolwork. Ivana Trump told Jennifer Steinhauer of the *New York Times* that Ivanka could not model when school was in session, but rather only on holidays and on the weekends.

Ivanka modeled clothing and high fashion outfits in shows for Versace, Marc Bouwer, and Thierry Mugler when she was fifteen. She also appeared on the

Ivanka worked with her father in the Trump Organization. In 2007, the Trumps announced the sale of condominium units in the Trump Soho Hotel Condominium. Construction on the New York City hotel was completed in 2010.

cover of *Seventeen* magazine in the May 1997 issue and was featured in an article in the issue about celebrity mothers and daughters. In 1997, Ivanka Trump also cohosted the Miss Teen USA pageant, an organization which her father co-owned at the time.

Ivanka considered modeling as a way to make some of her own money and to keep from being bored while away at boarding school in Connecticut. She recalled her modeling career in a *Marie Claire* article from January 29, 2007:

Modeling was not an endgame for me. I didn't particularly enjoy the act of it. It's as ruthless an industry as real estate—the people you meet in that business are just as ... tough. I used it as an excuse to travel. I used it as a way to break up the monotony. It was great, but it is an annoying source of confusion at this juncture in my life.

In 2005, Ivanka moved away from modeling and joined her father's business, the Trump Organization, as part of the development team. She went on to become vice president of real estate development and acquisitions and worked on development deals, planning, marketing, operations, sales, and leasing. In 2006, Ivanka Trump partnered with the Dynamic Diamond Corp to create her own branded line of fine jewelry.

CHAPTER 2

JARED: THE ORIGIN STORY

Like his future wife, Ivanka Trump, Jared Kushner grew up in an affluent family in the real estate business. Jared Corey Kushner was born on January 10, 1981. During his high school years, Kushner attended the Frisch School, a yeshiva, or Orthodox Jewish school, in Paramus, New Jersey. He graduated from the Frisch School in 1999. Jared next attended Harvard University and graduated in 2003 with a degree in government. He then went to graduate school at New York University (NYU), where he earned a master's degree for business and a law degree in 2007.

The Kushner family became wealthy because of their dealings in real estate, mainly those in the New Jersey area. In a 2016 interview with Steven Bertoni for *Forbes*, Kushner recalled spending time with his father growing up. He said, "My father never really believed in summer camp, so we'd come with him to the office … We'd go look at jobs, work on construction sites. It taught us real work."

JARED'S PARENTS

Jared Kushner comes from a large Modern Orthodox Jewish family with several siblings and an interesting historical family background.

Jared's mother, Seryl Stadtmauer, was born in 1954 in New Jersey. She attended the Stern College for Women in New York City. There is a dining hall at the school that is named in her honor. After graduating she then went on to acquire her master's degree in business administration at Hofstra University's Frank G. Zarb School of Business in Hempstead, New York. Seryl married Charles Kushner in 1974.

Jared's father, Charles Kushner, was born on May 16, 1954, in Elizabeth, New Jersey. Charles's mother, Rae, who was born in Poland, originally wanted to name him Chanan, after his uncle who died in the

> "
> My father never really believed in summer camp, so we'd come with him to the office ... We'd go look at jobs, work on construction sites. It taught us real work."
> —JARED KUSHNER

The Kushner family worked in real estate and other businesses. Jared (*center*) poses here with his father, Charles (*left*), and his mother, Seryl (*right*), while at an event for the *New York Observer* in 2007.

Holocaust during World War II. Because the nurse at his birth knew that Rae did not speak English very well, she told Rae that people in the United States did not use names like Chanan. Instead, the nurse gave him the name Charles. The family used the name Chanan as his Hebrew name. Charles attended New York University, where he received his bachelor's degree and an MBA. Afterward, he went to Hofstra and earned a law degree.

Both of Charles Kushner's parents survived the Holocaust in Europe during World War II. They immigrated to Brooklyn, New York, in 1949. Charles's father, Joseph, was a carpenter in Poland and found a job as a construction worker in the United States. After saving money he soon purchased some land with partners and built new houses and apartments in New Jersey. The builders with whom Joseph Kushner worked were known as the Holocaust builders because they survived the Holocaust during the war.

While growing up, Charles spent a lot of time with his father and his construction business. According to an interview with Lauren Elkies on therealdeal.com, Charles Kushner said, "I walked the construction sites with my father at like ten years old, and then I assumed different responsibilities within the context of what my father's work was [as an independent builder]. It ranged from being on job sites to attending business meetings."

Charles had started his own real estate company and partnered with his father just before Joseph died suddenly on October 5, 1985. Joseph Kushner had built four thousand apartments by that time. He left the apartments to Charles and his other son, Murray. Over the years, Charles grew the business he started with his father to more than twenty-five thousand apartments, as well as commercial real estate, industrial and retail space, hotels, and undeveloped land.

KUSHNER GRANDPARENTS-HOLOCAUST SURVIVORS

The Holocaust of World War II was a mass killing of six million European Jews and other minority groups between 1941 and 1945 by Nazi Germany. During the war, Jared Kushner's grandparents, Rae and Joseph Kushner, were living in the city of Novogrudok, which

(continued on the next page)

The Kushner family

Семья Кушнер

During World War II, German forces made Jared Kushner's relatives, pictured in this photograph, live in the Novogrudok ghetto, which is today part of Belarus.

(continued from the previous page)

is now part of the European country of Belarus. Rae was sixteen when the Germans invaded and massacred many people. Afterward, her family was forced to live in the Novogrudok ghetto. More executions followed and Rae's mother and a sister were killed.

When there were only around three hundred Jews left in the ghetto, the group decided to try to escape by digging a tunnel underneath the heavily guarded area. At night, they managed to dig a narrow 600-foot (183-meter) tunnel that led out into the woods. Out of about 250 people who escaped, only 170 survived. Many were killed by gunfire. Rae's brother, Chanan, was among those killed during the escape. The story of the famous uprising became the subject of the 2008 film *Defiance*, starring Daniel Craig and Liev Schreiber.

Those who became free eventually found the Bielski camp and survived a harsh life hiding until the war was over. After the war, Rae married Yossel Berkowitz. Because Yossel came from a poor family he took Rae's last name and became known as Joseph Kushner. They eventually immigrated to the United States in 1949.

While Jared was growing up, his father branched out of his real estate business and became more involved in politics. He often donated to the Democratic Party. Politicians such as Hillary Clinton would sometimes visit the spacious Kushner home in Livingston, New Jersey, seeking political contributions. In 2000, when Vice President Al Gore visited the Kushner home during Gore's presidential campaign, Jared Kushner was nineteen years old. Charles asked Jared to introduce Al Gore to the gathering of donors at his home that day. According to Andrew Rice's article for *New York* magazine, a Democratic officeholder from Livingston, Pat Sebold, was quoted as saying, "Charlie put Jared up there to do the talking ... I was impressed that he was a young guy and handled himself so well."

JARED KUSHNER'S SIBLINGS

Charles and Seryl Kushner have four children, Dara, Jared, Nicole, and Joshua, whom they raised in Livingston, New Jersey. The Kushner siblings grew up in a close-knit Jewish family in a large, eighteen-room mansion in Livingston, in a community that Kushner's grandfather and his associates helped build. The Jewish temple where they worshipped with many neighbors, friends, and business associates was within walking distance from their home.

Jared's oldest sister, Dara, was born February 12, 1979. She married David Orbach, who works as the chairman of Regal Bank in New Jersey. They have four children together. Dara is close with her family, but she does not work within the Kushner family businesses. In June 2017, Dara and her husband visited the Kushners at the White House. The Orbach children played with Jared and Ivanka's children, who are their cousins. The children were photographed playing together in the White House briefing room.

The second-born Kushner daughter, Nicole, was born on April 15, 1983. She attended NYU and earned a master's degree in urban planning in 2006. Like her sister, Dara, Nicole did not start her career in the Kushner family business. Instead, she chose to work in fashion. She worked for Ralph Lauren for about ten years and became a senior director of creative services at the company. Nicole is married to Joseph Meyer, a hedge fund manager and the CEO of Observer Media, the parent company of the *New York Observer*, which Jared Kushner purchased in 2006. Nicole later joined the family business, Kushner Companies, in 2015.

Jared Kushner's youngest sibling, Joshua, was born on June 12, 1985. Like Jared, Joshua also attended Harvard University. He also attended Harvard Business School. After graduating he made money by investing in internet companies such as Kickstarter and GroupMe. By investing in the companies so they can operate, he can receive money back when those companies succeed. In 2010, he started his own company, Thrive Capital. It invests in new companies, such as Harry's, a company that makes razors, and the eyeglasses company Warby Parker. Thrive Capital also invested in the social media photo sharing app Instagram. Joshua Kushner was featured on

Jared (*left*) and his brother, Joshua (*right*), pose with their mother, Seryl, at the Library Lions Gala on November 3, 2014, in New York City.

the April 25, 2017, issue of *Forbes*. In July 2018, he got engaged to model Karlie Kloss.

JARED AT HARVARD

Jared Kushner left the Frisch School and his family in Livingston in the fall of 1999 when he moved to Cambridge, Massachusetts, after being accepted into Harvard University, one of the most prestigious universities in the world.

It has been suggested in media reports that Kushner did not get into Harvard on his academic merits alone. The 2006 book by Pulitzer Prize–winning writer Daniel Golden, *The Price of Admission*, details how many wealthy families use money, power, influence, and political connections to help their children gain access to elite universities. In his book, Golden wrote:

> New Jersey real estate developer Charles Kushner had pledged $2.5 million to Harvard University in 1998, not long before his son Jared was admitted to the prestigious Ivy League school. At the time, Harvard accepted about one of every nine applicants. (Nowadays, it only takes one out of twenty.)

Even though there was controversy surrounding Kushner's acceptance into Harvard, he was very busy while at school there, not just with his studies but with his own business dealings. Charles Kushner continually sent business documents to Jared throughout his first year at school. When he had just finished his freshman year and was only nineteen years old, he was already purchasing various properties around Massachusetts, altogether worth more than $9 million.

In 2004, while still in school and interning for a Manhattan district attorney, Jared was thrust into the family business when his father was arrested for tax evasion, election fraud, and witness tampering.

Charles Kushner remained free on $5 million bail until his prison sentence began on May 9, 2005. He also had to pay a $40,000 fine. Jared

BUYING THE *NEW YORK OBSERVER*

In 2006, while still studying for his degrees in business and law at NYU, Kushner purchased the *New York Observer* for $10 million. The *Observer* was an elite paper with a small circulation at the time. It was known for the salmon-pink paper on which it was printed. Kushner was twenty-five years old at the time of the purchase. Karl Vick quoted Arthur Mirante II, a business consultant and friend of Kushner, in an article in *Time* magazine, saying, "His graduation present was the *Observer*."

The *Observer* had been in print from 1987 to 2014 when Kushner decided to make the paper available only online. Kushner made other changes, too, like bringing in a new editor and asking politicians to write columns.

Shortly after buying the *Observer*, Jared met and began dating Ivanka Trump. The *Observer* eventually became one of the first news organizations to endorse Donald Trump during the Republican primary in 2016.

visited his father weekly during his time in prison. Charles wound up spending more than a year in federal prison at the Montgomery County Correctional Facility in Alabama. He served the remaining time at a halfway house in Newark, New

Kushner's father, Charles (*second from left*), was arrested in 2004. He, his wife, Seryl, and his legal team are surrounded by the media as they enter the US District Courthouse in Newark, New Jersey, in August 2004.

Jersey, before being released in August 2006.

According to Gabriel Sherman's July 12, 2009, article in *New York* magazine, Charles Kushner said, "[Jared] was the best son to his father in jail ... the best son to his mother, who suffered terribly, and he was a father to his siblings."

Despite everything that was going on, Jared Kushner graduated from NYU in 2007 with master's degrees in both business and law.

CHAPTER 3

MEETING OF THE MINDS

By 2007, Ivanka Trump and Jared Kushner had both graduated from college and entered the working world as important contributors to their fathers' businesses. Each was making a mark as an important and influential person.

Trump was already working for her father's organization as the vice president of real estate development and acquisitions and launching her own fashion brand, Ivanka Trump Jewelry Collection. Kushner had taken over many aspects of the multibillion-dollar Kushner family business

Jared Kushner bought the *New York Observer*, a weekly newspaper, in 2006. The paper became an online-only newspaper called the Observer in late 2016.

and was the owner of the influential newspaper the *New York Observer.*

So how did this power couple meet? They met over a business lunch to discuss a possible real estate deal. They were both twenty-five years old when they were introduced to each other at the Prime Grill steakhouse in Manhattan. The meeting took place across the street from Trump Tower and was arranged by Ivanka's business partner, Moshe Lax, and another friend.

In an interview with Jonathan Van Meter for *Vogue* magazine, Trump recalled their first meeting: "They very innocently set us up thinking that our only interest in one another would be transactional … Whenever we see them we're like: *The best deal we ever made!*"

When Trump and Kushner first started dating, the press began speculating immediately and several short media write-ups began appearing in *New York* magazine and the *New York Post*'s gossip column, Page Six. According to the article "Oh, J-Vanka!" in *New York* magazine, the two were seen kissing in May 2007 at a bowling alley, Bowlmor Lanes, in Manhattan. Soon after, in April 2007, Kushner threw a party at the Four Seasons hotel in Manhattan for his newly acquired newspaper the *New York Observer*. The next day, on April 19, news of Ivanka Trump being seen with Kushner at the party appeared in nymag.com. At the time, despite the media not knowing whether they were even dating, they were already being referred to in print as "J-Vanka."

The news reports continued for months, and an article on June 7, 2007, in *New York* magazine playfully reported on another event where the two were seen together—at the Art Party of the Whitney Museum of American Art in Manhattan. The press reported everything about the couple, even what they wore. According to that *New York* magazine article:

> Ivanka arrived wearing a little black dress that she said was vintage. She posed for photos ... Fifteen minutes later, the Kush arrived, wearing a blue blazer, white shirt open at the neck, and loosened tie. Tight black jeans, too, and driving mocs with no socks. A publicist walked him in front of the backdrop to pose for photos.

Again in October 2007 they were spotted together at a Maroon 5 rock concert at Madison Square Garden. Eventually Ivanka Trump finally confirmed that she was dating Jared Kushner in a *New York Times* article on December 27, 2007.

THE BREAKUP

Ivanka Trump and Jared Kushner stopped dating at one point and broke up, reportedly because of a conflict about religious observances. Jared Kushner comes from a Modern Orthodox Jewish family and Ivanka Trump comes from a Presbyterian family. Modern Orthodox Jews are not allowed to marry people who are not of the same faith. Rather than continue dating, the couple broke up in the summer of 2008.

While they were dating, Ivanka Trump and Jared Kushner were continually followed and reported on by tabloid newspapers. Here, they make an appearance at the *Vanity Fair* and Tribeca Film Festival Party in 2007.

News reports commented on their power, wealth, and good looks when reporting about the bad news of their breakup. On April 2, 2008, in *New York* magazine, the Daily Intelligencer reported:

> They. Are. Too. Attractive. To. Break. Up … They're both bajillionaires with Ivy League educations who are nine feet tall and thin. And they're funny and charming, too. IF THEY CAN'T MAKE IT WORK IN THIS CITY, NOBODY CAN. We've reached out to them for comment and will let you know if this all isn't true. If it is, we're moving to Tallahassee.

Also, according to Lizzie Widdicombe's article in the *New Yorker*, Jared's friend Nitin Saigal said, "I know he loved Ivanka dearly … But the religious thing was important to him."

The breakup did not last long. Jared and Ivanka were invited separately, without the other knowing, for a weekend getaway party on a 184-foot (57-m) yacht, the *Rosehearty*, which was owned by media mogul billionaire Rupert Murdoch and his wife at the time, Wendi Deng Murdoch. The weekend on the yacht turned out to be a success. Trump and Kushner started dating again and decided they would eventually like to get engaged. Before actually becoming officially engaged, however, Ivanka needed to convert to Modern Orthodox Judaism.

ENGAGEMENT AND WEDDING

Trump took the process of converting to Judaism very seriously and studied with a rabbi at a synagogue in New York City. She chose the Hebrew name *Yael*, which means, "strength of God."

In a July 12, 2009, article in *New York* magazine, Ivanka said, "I am studying … and it's been an amazing and fulfilling experience for me."

After Trump finished her conversion to Judaism, on July 15, 2009, she and Kushner became engaged. Kushner gave Trump a 5.22-carat cushion-cut diamond with a platinum and diamond mounting that he helped design. The ring design would later be included in Ivanka's own jewelry line, Ivanka Trump Fine Jewelry. The following day, Trump announced their engagement on her Twitter feed, "I got engaged last night … truly the happiest day of my life!!!"

The Trump-Kushner wedding took place on October 25, 2009, at the Trump National Golf Club in Bedminster, New Jersey. Trump was twenty-seven and Kushner was twenty-eight. There were five hundred guests and several celebrities and high-profile people at the wedding, such as Barbara Walters, Rupert Murdoch, Regis Philbin, Corey Booker, Anna Wintour, Russell Crowe, and Natalie Portman. Politicians such as New York City Mayor Rudy Giuliani and then–attorney general of New York Andrew Cuomo also attended.

CONVERTING TO MODERN ORTHODOX JUDAISM

Before their official engagement could even be announced, Ivanka Trump converted to Jared Kushner's religion, Modern Orthodox Judaism. Converting one's religion to Judaism is a big decision and often requires a person to make many life changes. The changes are not just with a person's beliefs but also with changes to diet, observation of holidays, and day-to-day cultural traditions.

After converting to Judaism, Ivanka Trump started eating in the Kosher tradition, which requires special food preparation and food restrictions. Certain types of meat, such as pork, rabbit, kangaroo, and fox, may not be eaten.

Kosher foods are classified as either meat, dairy, or pareve. Meat and dairy products may not be cooked or eaten together. Pareve refers to "neutral" foods, because they can be eaten with either dairy or meat products.

As a Modern Orthodox Jewish family, the Kushners also observe the weekly ritual of Sabbath. The Sabbath tradition (also called Shabbat, or Shabbos) is a twenty-

> [Ivanka] became a great cook. So, for Friday, she'll make dinner for just the two of us, and we turn our phones off for 25 hours. Putting aside the religious aspect of it; we live in such a fast-paced world."
>
> —JARED KUSHNER

five-hour period of rest that comes at the end of every week. It is observed from just before sunset on Friday to nightfall the following day, on Saturday. The weekly ritual centers on rest, family, and home life with family, friends, and guests. Driving a car and the use of all electronics is not allowed.

Sabbath begins with a candle-lighting ceremony, prayer with wine, and a family meal of traditional foods. The Sabbath can also be observed at temple with family and friends.

As revealed in Jonathan Van Meter's article in *Vogue* magazine, Kushner said, "[Ivanka] became a great cook. So, for Friday, she'll make dinner for just the two of us, and we turn our phones off for 25 hours. Putting aside the religious aspect of it; we live in such a fast-paced world."

The bridesmaids at the wedding were Trump's half-sister, Tiffany, and her sister-in-law, Vanessa Trump. Trump's brother, Barron, who was three years old at the time, was the ring bearer. Famous fashion designer Vera Wang designed Trump's wedding dress.

The wedding cake at the event was thirteen layers and 70 inches (178 centimeters) in height, with chocolate, carrot, almond, and yellow cake flavors throughout. Custom cake designer Sylvia Weinstock described the cake she made to Sharon Cotliar of *People* magazine. Weinstock explained,

Ivanka Trump and Jared Kushner pose for a formal photograph on their wedding day, October 25, 2009, at the Trump National Golf Club in Bedminster, New Jersey.

"Each layer was ringed with flowers. We had lisianthus, roses, peonies, lilies of the valley, baby's breath—all in the coloring of whites, creams, pinks, ivory, and flush tones."

A few days after the wedding, Trump and Kushner set off for a safari honeymoon in South Africa. Trump kept her Twitter followers updated with informative tweets and photos during the honeymoon.

CHAPTER 4

THE YIN AND YANG OF TRUMP AND KUSHNER

Since they met, Ivanka Trump and Jared Kushner naturally focused their efforts, individually and as a couple, on business. Less than a decade after getting married, they also had three children together. Living in Manhattan, Trump and Kushner continually came in and out of the media spotlight regarding real estate deals, publishing and book deals, fashion, television, and, eventually, politics. Trump, like her father, gravitated toward the media spotlight, while Kushner mainly avoided it.

Ivanka Trump showcases a necklace and earrings at an event at the Trump Taj Mahal Hotel Casino in Atlantic City, New Jersey, to launch her jewelry line.

IVANKA TRUMP BRAND

Until 2005, Trump had been working as the vice president of real estate development and acquisitions of her father's company, the Trump Organization. She arranged and oversaw many of the organization's real estate deals. Some of these deals included the purchase of a large property in Miami, Florida, and an agreement to convert the Old Post Office and Clock Tower building on Pennsylvania Avenue in Washington, DC, into a luxury hotel.

In 2006, Ivanka Trump decided to start a business of her own. She soon partnered with the Dynamic Diamond Corp to create her own branded line of fine jewelry. In 2007, Ivanka Trump Fine Jewelry was launched as well as a new boutique bearing her name on Madison Avenue in New York City.

Jared Kushner facilitated the Kushner Companies' acquisition of the New York City skyscraper 666 Fifth Avenue (*center*) in early 2007. The $1.8 billion real estate deal was a record at the time.

According to an article on HamiltonJewelers.com, Trump was quoted as saying, "This jewelry will appeal to women who have a strong sense of themselves, value exquisite craftsmanship and wear even the most important fine jewelry with a kind of off-handed elegance ... My female customers have a sense of tradition [and] appreciate quality."

In 2011, Trump went on to launch a clothing line that sold in department stores such as Macy's, Hudson's Bay, and Lord & Taylor. Trump's jewelry and clothing lines were successful and contributed to the wealth of her new family. In the fall of 2011, Trump moved her flagship store from Madison Avenue to SoHo.

TRUMP AND KUSHNER PHILANTHROPY

Before meeting, the Trump and Kushner families each engaged in philanthropy, which is the act of giving or donating to groups or causes that need assistance, especially to help promote human welfare.

Kushner's parents donated money to start the Joseph Kushner Hebrew Academy and Rae Kushner Yeshiva High School. The Kushner family has also supported the Ramaz School and the Solomon Schechter School of Manhattan and Yeshiva University.

Trump's father created The Donald J. Trump Foundation in 1987 with funds he earned from his bestselling book *The Art of the Deal.* Since its creation, the foundation has given away millions of dollars to schools, the United Way, and many museums. In late 2018, President Trump began dissolving the foundation and planned to distribute the remaining money to various charities.

Like their parents, Trump and Kushner have given money to causes and organizations they support. Some of the organizations Ivanka Trump has supported include AIDS LIFE, Children's Aid Society, Habitat for Humanity, Operation Smile, St. Jude Children's Hospital, United Cerebral Palsy, and the Walkabout Foundation. Trump and Kushner have both donated to a number of Jewish charities that include Chai Lifeline, Mikvaot, and United Hatzalah.

When Trump and Kushner married in 2009 they asked their guests to contribute to a charity of their choice rather than give the couple wedding gifts.

666 FIFTH AVENUE

In early 2007, just before meeting Ivanka Trump and not long after taking control of his father's family business, Jared Kushner closed a deal on the purchase of a New York City skyscraper. It was, and continues to be, the largest real estate deal of his life. It was also the most expensive building purchase in US history at the time—$1.8 billion.

When the Kushner Companies first began to pursue the acquisition of 666 Fifth Avenue in February 2006, Kushner's father, Charles, was still in prison. Once Charles was released in August 2006, he helped his son with the deal behind the scenes. Jared was to be the new face of Kushner Companies, and he worked hard to close his first big real estate deal and signal himself as an important player in Manhattan real estate.

On Friday, January 12, 2007, Kushner Companies finalized the deal and purchased the property. The news of the $1.8 billion deal was not announced to the press until January 30, 2007.

Kushner, in a January 30 *New York Observer* press release, said:

> We're pleased to expand the Kushner portfolio in Manhattan with the addition of such a unique asset. We are very bullish on New York real estate, and we are confident that 666 Fifth has great upside potential. We identified a premier building with the highest quality

office configuration and one of the best retail boxes in the world.

In October 2007, just after the deal was finalized, Adam Piore interviewed Kushner on realdeal.com. In the interview Kushner said, "I love New York—it's the greatest city in the world. In this particular transaction, we bought really the center of the world, Fifth Avenue and 52nd Street. It doesn't get any better than that."

The purchase of 666 Fifth Avenue was very prestigious and newsworthy, but it also meant the Kushner Companies would owe a lot of money to make the payments. The purchase was made in the hopes that retail and commercial rental prices in New York City would go up and help the company make a profit in the coming years. Unfortunately, the following year, in 2008, the world economy suffered the largest financial crisis since the Great Depression in the 1930s. The housing market collapsed, stock prices for companies fell sharply, and the Dow Jones Industrial Average lost more than a third of its value in one year.

By April 2008, Kushner Companies was losing money quickly on the building. To help the problem, Jared Kushner sold 49 percent of the retail space in the building for $525 million. Because of the sale, the building could continue to serve as the main office for Kushner Companies in the years to follow. On August 3, 2018, however, Brookfield Properties

Ivanka Trump and Jared Kushner pose at a party with the acclaimed fashion designer Narciso Rodriguez (*center*) to launch the designer's 2008 clothing line.

announced they had acquired the leasing rights of 666 Fifth Avenue for ninety-nine years. The financial details were not disclosed but the deal allowed Kushner Companies enough funds to pay off their $1.1 billion of debt on the property.

PUBLIC AND PRIVATE FAMILY LIFE

Although Kushner has been interviewed, he gives interviews rarely, and he typically talks about business and less about family life. He also does not use social media to communicate to the public. Trump, on the other hand, grew up with the media, became a model as a teen, and has been less shy about taking interviews and revealing personal details about the Trump and Kushner home life on social media sites like Twitter and Instagram.

A PUBLIC IVANKA

Ivanka Trump enjoys sharing a more public life than her husband. She has been interviewed many times and often posts on social media sites. As of December 2018, her Twitter account had 6 million followers and more than fourteen thousand tweets. Her Instagram account had 4.7 million followers and she had posted more than three thousand photos on the site.

Just prior to her engagement to Kushner, in Gabriel Sherman's July 17, 2007, *New York* magazine article, Trump explained details of their day-to-day lives. She said:

> We're very mellow. We go to the park. We go biking together. We go to the 2nd Avenue Deli. We both live in this fancy world. But on a personal level, I don't think I could be with somebody—I know he couldn't be with somebody—who needed to be "on" all the time ... I don't think we've ever been to a nightclub together in two years ... I'm really thankful for that. I have a lot of stamina, but I

don't think I have the stamina to work as hard as I do and play that hard.

After getting married, Trump and Kushner decided to wait about one year and enjoy some time being married before having their first child. Between the years 2011 and 2016, Trump and Kushner had three children. While pregnant with their first child, Trump and Kushner moved from Kushner's old Greenwich Village apartment into a four-bedroom penthouse apartment on Park Avenue and 59th Street. The penthouse apartment was owned by Donald Trump.

Prior to the birth of her first child, Trump was executive vice president of development and acquisition at her father's company as well as a host on the NBC reality show *The Celebrity Apprentice*. Trump first started appearing on her father's reality TV show, *The Apprentice*, in 2006 as a host. According to the Internet Movie Database (IMDB), she was involved with the show from 2006 to 2015 and appeared on many episodes and also served as a boardroom judge. The reality show featured aspiring businesspeople and entrepreneurs. Judges rated the business plans and performances of the "apprentices" on the show. The participants were eliminated with the catch phrase that Donald Trump used to make the show popular, *"You're fired."*

In addition to her career working for the Trump Organization she was also boardroom judge for

Ivanka Trump (*right*) began working alongside her father (*left*) on his hit reality television show, *The Apprentice*, in 2006. She was a boardroom judge on the show until it ended in 2015.

the *The Apprentice* from the show's sixth season until it ended in 2015. Trump also wrote her first book, *The Trump Card: Playing to Win in Work and Life*, which was published in 2009.

In an interview with Julie Vadnal in *ELLE* magazine, Trump was asked why she wrote the book:

> After being on *The Apprentice*, I got so many letters from young people who wanted basic career advice. How do I get hired faster? How do you lay the foundation for a successful

career? And there really wasn't anything that spoke to people in a peer-to-peer-type way. Everything was told from the vantage point of a 70-year-old man reflecting on a long corporate career.

In May and June 2011, just before having her first child, Trump spoke with Elisa Lipsky-Karasz for *Harper's Bazaar* and Jeremy W. Peters of the *New York Times* about her and Kushner's family life. The articles described Kushner and Trump staying at home on Friday evenings and preparing for the weekly Jewish Sabbath. Trump, who had not cooked much prior to her conversion to Judaism, would often cook dishes like Moroccan meat pie and sweet pea soup. On Saturdays she and Kushner would sometimes go out for simple meals like pizza.

Their first child, a daughter named Arabella Rose Kushner, was born on July 17, 2011. On her Twitter feed, Trump announced Arabella's birth, welcoming their new baby girl into the world. Trump also expressed how grateful and blessed she and Kushner both felt.

> "After being on *The Apprentice*, I got so many letters from young people who wanted basic career advice. How do I get hired faster? How do you lay the foundation for a successful career? And there really wasn't anything that spoke to people in a peer-to-peer-type way."
>
> **—IVANKA TRUMP**

A PRIVATE KUSHNER

Despite his tendency to be the opposite of his wife in regard to the media spotlight, Kushner has still stepped into it at times. In 2010, Trump and Kushner made a cameo appearance together on the TV show *Gossip Girl* in an episode called "Easy J," in which they played themselves.

Kushner does not engage with social media to the same extent as his wife. He started a Twitter account in 2009 and has more than sixty-three thousand followers, but he has not posted a single tweet. He does not have an Instagram account. Kushner rarely speaks publicly and typically is quoted speaking only on business topics.

In 2011, Kushner was still working on modifying the Kushner Companies' loans for the 666 Fifth Avenue building in an effort to make it profitable. At the same time, Kushner had already replaced the *New York Observer*'s editor-in-chief as well as much of the staff. The newspaper would go through many more changes in the years to follow, including ending its print run in 2016 and becoming an online-only publication, called the *Observer.*

In 2012, Kushner attempted to buy the Los Angeles Dodgers baseball team. The Dodgers began as a New York City baseball team before moving to Los Angeles in 1957. Had Kushner successfully purchased the team he would have been the youngest person to own a baseball team. He was thirty-one years old at the time, but he eventually withdrew his bid in March 2012.

Later in 2012, Kushner had moved back into more real estate acquisitions. In August 2012, Kushner purchased more than 5,500 rental apartments in Baltimore, Maryland.

On October 14, 2013, Trump and Kushner's second child was born, a son, Joseph Frederick Kushner. The following day, Ivanka Trump tweeted the announcement: "We just welcomed a beautiful & healthy son into the world. Jared, Arabella and I couldn't be happier!" On March 27, 2016, at the height of Donald Trump's presidential campaign, the couple's third child, Theodore James, was born.

The couple worked hard to balance their family and work lives. Once Trump's father won the US presidency, it became even more of a struggle to balance their lives with three small children. Trump and Kushner eventually moved their family from New York City to Washington, DC.

CHAPTER 5

YOU'RE HIRED! DONALD TRUMP WINS PRESIDENCY

Donald Trump had mentioned the idea of running for president of the United States several times before he first announced his bid for the White House in the election of 2016. In the Lipsky-Karasz interview with *Harper's Bazaar*, Ivanka spoke about the possibility of her father running for office one day. She pointed out his business experience as a reason he would be a good president. "I think he's exactly what we need … He's the best equipped to deal with the most important issues this nation has, which is ultimately that we're suffering under a massive burden of debt. We need a very acute financial mind to get us out of this mire."

On June 6, 2015, Ivanka Trump announced her father's candidacy for the US presidency at Trump Tower. Ivanka was very involved in her father's presidential campaign.

Several years later, on June 16, 2015, Donald Trump officially announced he was running for president of the United States. The announcement was made at a press conference in his building, Trump Tower. Reporter Tierney McAfee, in *People*, quoted Trump as saying, "So, ladies and gentlemen, I am officially running for president of the United States, and we are going to make our country great again." The same day he also tweeted the news and introduced the hashtag that would become his campaign slogan: Make America Great Again.

Ivanka Trump and Jared Kushner had been moving in their own direction as a power couple for many years in both real estate and retail. Soon Donald Trump's presidential campaign would require the help of his entire extended family and propel them all into the world of politics.

IVANKA TRUMP: FRONT-AND-CENTER CAMPAIGN SPOKESPERSON

As soon as Donald Trump announced he was running for president as a Republican candidate, his daughter and son-in-law became integral parts of his campaign. Both Trump and Kushner had been supporters of the Democratic Party. Ivanka Trump was in the spotlight from the beginning, while Jared Kushner, despite his integral role in the campaign, operated mostly behind the scenes.

Ivanka Trump introduced her father at Trump Tower when he first announced he was running for president. On C-SPAN, Trump said, "Welcome everybody. Today I have the honor of introducing a man who needs no introduction. His legend has been built, and his accomplishments are too many to name. That man is my father." After speaking at length, Trump then concluded her six-minute introduction, "Ladies and gentlemen. It is my pleasure to introduce to you today a man who I have loved and respected my entire life. My father, Donald J. Trump."

CAMPAIGN BABIES

In 2016, Hillary Clinton of the Democratic Party made history when she became the first woman to win a party nomination as a candidate for president of the United States. While Donald Trump and Hillary Clinton battled on the campaign trail to become president, their daughters Ivanka Trump and her friend Chelsea Clinton were each expecting a child. Trump was pregnant with her third child, and Clinton was pregnant with her second. On March 27, 2016, Ivanka Trump gave birth to her and Kushner's third child, Theodore James Kushner. Less than three months later, on June 18, 2016, Clinton and her husband, Marc Mezvinsky, welcomed their son, Aidan.

Trump and Clinton had been friends for years before their parents ran against each other for president. They had promised to stay friends after the campaign, and even planned to get their sons together for play dates.

According to the *Detroit News*, Donald Trump described his daughter as "his most trusted adviser" and explained "Anybody that Ivanka likes, I like."

Donald Trump's campaign for president was often very controversial and heated, with Trump himself speaking bluntly with his critics and with reporters. Ivanka Trump was instrumental throughout the campaign, often acting as spokesperson to defend her father along the way. Trump traveled with her father, helping him appeal to younger voters and to women.

On April 16, 2016, in the *New York Times*, Trump defended her father: "What bothers me is how rash people are to make claims as if they knew him and they knew his viewpoint on certain topics," she said. "My father has an enormous heart and truly loves people—all people."

Donald Trump valued and respected his daughter's opinion throughout the campaign. Ivanka Trump traveled around the country with her father, going to political rallies, polling stations, and senior citizen centers. She also helped start Trump's campaign headquarters in New Hampshire and recorded a TV commercial for him in Iowa about the election process. Trump even shared some late-evening food with her father when he periodically ordered McDonald's food.

> "
> What bothers me is how rash people are to make claims as if they knew him and they knew his viewpoint on certain topics ... My father has an enormous heart and truly loves people—all people."
>
> —IVANKA TRUMP

JARED KUSHNER: BEHIND-THE-SCENES CAMPAIGN STRATEGIST

Jared Kushner was instrumental in helping his father-in-law win the Republican nomination as well as the presidency. From behind the scenes, Kushner was a trusted insider and adviser to Donald Trump throughout the campaign.

In *Newsweek*, Trump campaign spokesperson Hope Hicks confirmed that Kushner had no official role in the campaign but that he did help Trump arrange meetings, including one with US

Rarely seen in front of the cameras, Jared Kushner (*right*) worked mostly behind the scenes on his father-in-law's presidential campaign. During the campaign, Kushner was a close adviser to Donald Trump.

senator Jeff Sessions. Kushner helped Donald Trump make plans for a trip to Israel in 2015, but the trip was eventually canceled. Kushner also assisted in writing campaign speeches for Trump and organized people to write speeches and propose possible policies. He also organized Trump's busy schedule and managed the campaign finances.

As the Trump campaign progressed, Kushner took on more and more responsibility and much of it was not known until after Donald Trump won the presidential election against the Democratic candidate, Hillary Clinton. Kushner never had an official role title on the campaign, but along the way he convinced Trump to use social media to help drive his campaign goals. Kushner used his business and publishing

Donald Trump won the election against Hillary Clinton to become the forty-fifth president of the United States. Ivanka Trump and Jared Kushner congratulated him after his acceptance speech in the early morning of November 9, 2016.

experience, along with some technical help from his information technology friends in California to craft target marketing on the internet.

After Trump won the election, in a December 2016 article in *Forbes*, Kushner explained how he approached some of his digital marketing friends in Silicon Valley, California, asking for advice on how to utilize the internet strategically during the campaign. He also explained how he was given a tutorial on how to use Facebook for micro-targeting different audiences.

According to *Forbes*, Kushner's strategy paid off, and the campaign increased sales of Trump hats from a couple of thousand dollars to around $80,000 very quickly. Kushner also employed the use of a political data company, Cambridge Analytica, as well as the Republican National Committee's data, to target specific voters with political ads in places that mattered, such as swing states. This strategy helped keep costs down so the campaign would not waste money. *Forbes* also reported that an additional $250 million came in from individuals and small donors using similar strategies. Despite Donald Trump's being a billionaire, Kushner's behind-the-scenes tech-savvy strategy for the campaign allowed the Trump campaign to spend half as much as Hillary Clinton's campaign and still win the election.

Former Google CEO Eric Schmidt worked on the technology system for Hillary Clinton's campaign. Schmidt said in 2016 in *Forbes*:

Jared understood the online world in a way the traditional media folks didn't. He managed to assemble a presidential campaign on a shoestring [budget] using new technology and won. That's a big deal ... Remember all those articles about how they had no money, no people, organizational structure? Well, they won, and Jared ran it.

Another way Kushner aided the campaign was by concentrating his efforts on helping Trump win the Electoral College vote rather than the popular vote. In the US presidential voting system, each state has a vote in the electors of its state. To win the election, a candidate needs at least 270 electoral votes. With a total of 538 available, Kushner helped Trump concentrate on the states with the largest number of electoral votes to reach 270. This focus led Trump to a win, despite Clinton's capture of the popular vote by almost three million.

CHAPTER 6

ADVISERS TO THE PRESIDENT

Many newsmakers and political strategists believed Hillary Clinton would win the 2016 election. On November 8, 2016, Donald J. Trump won a stunning Electoral College victory against Hillary Clinton, a former first lady, US senator, and US secretary of state, to become the forty-fifth president of the United States.

The transition of power between an incoming and outgoing president takes time. After Trump won the

On January 20, 2017, Donald Trump (*far left*) takes the oath of office as president of the United States as his family watches (*from left to right*: wife Melania, son Barron, daughter Ivanka, son Eric, and daughter Tiffany).

election on November 8, 2016, he had to work quickly to start the transition before taking the oath of office on January 20, 2017.

A presidential transition team is a group of people that makes recommendations to the incoming president about who to choose for the new administration. The job of the transition team is to recommend people to fill more than four thousand jobs in the administration. This

JEWISH "FIRST GRANDCHILDREN"

The election of Donald Trump made the Kushner family more than just White House advisers. The Kushner family's role as "first family" to the president meant that the United States had the first Jewish "first family" in its history. Donald Trump's grandchildren Arabella, Joseph, and Theodore are the first Jewish grandchildren of a sitting president. Although the grandchildren do not live in the White House, Trump and Kushner bring their children to the White House periodically to visit. As a family, they take part in celebrations open to other White House staff and employees, such as holiday parties.

procedure includes helping the president choose cabinet members, White House staff members, and policy and management positions at various federal agencies. The team is responsible for operations and support throughout the new period of presidential operations. The team's members are also in charge of helping to decide what policies should be put in place when the new president comes to office.

Donald Trump's children, Donald Trump Jr., Eric Trump, and Ivanka Trump, and his son-in-law, Jared Kushner, were all members of the Presidential

Transition Team Executive Committee. Ivanka Trump and Kushner continued to have central roles helping the president transition into the White House and advising him throughout his presidency. They both severed ties with their businesses as they transitioned into politics and a new life in Washington, DC. As advisers, dealmakers, and political insiders, Trump and Kushner's new roles in politics were both controversial and helpful to President Trump, who has continued to keep his daughter and son-in-law closer to him than perhaps anyone else in the White House.

As senior advisers to the president, Ivanka Trump and Jared Kushner attended the 2017 White House Christmas tree lighting ceremony with their children, Theodore, Arabella, and Joseph.

IVANKA, ADVISER TO THE PRESIDENT

> When my father takes office as the 45th President of the United States of America, I will take a formal leave of absence from The Trump Organization and my eponymous apparel and accessories brand. I will no longer be involved with the management or operations of either company."
>
> —IVANKA TRUMP

Ivanka Trump was not immediately appointed to any official position within the White House, but she did vow to quit her job at the Trump Organization as well as her position at her own company, Ivanka Trump Fine Jewelry. Her immediate plans before the inauguration included moving to Washington, DC, and finding a new home for the Kushner family.

On January 11, 2017, just nine days before her father took the oath of office, Ivanka Trump posted a statement on her Facebook page that said, "When my father takes office as the 45th President of the United States of America, I will take a formal leave of absence from The Trump Organization and my eponymous apparel and accessories brand. I will no longer be involved with the management or operations of either company."

After the Trump inauguration, the Kushners moved to the historic upscale residential neighborhood of Kalorama in Washington, DC. After leaving office, President Barack Obama's family moved to the same neighborhood, not far from the new Kushner home. Amazon CEO Jeff Bezos also has a home in the neighborhood.

Trump soon started working in an unofficial role in the White House, helping her father. After ethics concerns were raised, an official announcement was made on March 28, 2017, that Trump would serve as special assistant to the president with her own office in the West Wing.

Trump and Kushner's official roles as advisers to the president were unconventional. Although a president can get advice from family members, it is uncommon for a daughter or a son-in-law to take official roles in a president's administration. In the *New York Times* on March 29, 2017, Ivanka Trump responded to the controversy by stating:

> I have heard the concerns some have with my advising the president in my personal capacity while voluntarily complying with all ethics rules, and I will instead serve as an unpaid employee in the White House Office, subject to all of the same rules as other federal employees … Throughout this process I have been working closely and in good faith with the White House counsel and my personal counsel to address the unprecedented nature of my role.

There have been more than a dozen adult children of United States presidents who worked in different jobs for their parents while they were in serving in office. Many of them had various jobs or duties, but Ivanka Trump has an official role in serving the

JAVANKA–NAME BLENDING OF POWER COUPLES

Name blending of couples may seem like a recent phenomenon in the media, but the tradition goes back decades. In 1950, actors Desi Arnaz and Lucille Ball were married and formed the production company Desilu Productions, using a combination of their first names. They became famous for the 1950s television comedy I Love Lucy.

In 2002, after actors Ben Affleck and Jennifer Lopez began dating, the term Bennifer was coined by the media. A few of the more memorable power couple names are Kimye (Kim Kardashian West and Kanye West), Billary (Bill and Hillary Clinton), and Brady-Bundch (Tom Brady and Gisele Bundchen). Even after power couples break up, their names tend to stick, as in the cases of Brangelina (Brad Pitt and Angelina Jolie) and TomKat (Tom Cruise and Katie Holmes).

It was shortly after President Trump took office that the name Javanka was coined in the media to refer to Ivanka Trump and Jared Kushner.

president, which allows her to have a great influence on affecting policy.

To avoid criticism of nepotism, which is when relatives or friends are placed into positions

Ivanka Trump's second book, *Women Who Work: Rewriting the Rules for Success*, was published in 2017. All proceeds from the publication were donated to various charities.

of power, Trump and Kushner both agreed to work for President Trump for free. On March 30, 2017, on CNN.com, chief presidential campaign spokesperson Jason Miller was asked if Trump's appointment in the White House was nepotism. Miller replied, "She's working for free. She's volunteering her time and effort for the good of the country. Everybody from the White House counsel to the (Department of Justice) has said that this doesn't violate any sort of nepotism rules."

The debate in the media persisted and Ivanka Trump continued to take steps to ensure there were no conflicts of interest. Before the campaign had started, Trump had been working on a business book, *Women Who Work: Rewriting the Rules for Success*. It was set to be released on May 2, 2017. Before the book's release, Trump announced that to avoid any conflicts of interest, she would not be promoting the book and would donate all the book's proceeds to charity. Even her advance from the publisher was donated to charity. The Ivanka M. Trump Foundation was formed to receive any profits from the book after its release. The National Urban League and Boys & Girls Clubs of America were named as the first organizations to receive donations from the foundation.

On April 20, 2017, Trump posted a statement about the upcoming book on her Facebook page. In it she said, "Out of an abundance of caution and to avoid the appearance of using my official role to promote the book, I will not publicize the book through a promotional tour or media appearances."

KUSHNER, ADVISER TO THE PRESIDENT

Kushner also took an important role advising President Trump. On January 8, 2017, it was announced that Jared Kushner would take an official position in President Trump's administration as a senior White House adviser. According to TheHill.com, President Trump issued a statement in which he said, "Jared has been a tremendous asset and trusted adviser throughout the campaign and transition and I am proud to have him in a key leadership role in my administration ... He has been incredibly successful, in both business

Ivanka Trump (*second from left*) and Jared Kushner (*second from right*) attend President Trump's (*fourth from right*) first meeting with German chancellor Angela Merkel (*third from left*) at the White House in 2017.

and now politics. He will be an invaluable member of my team as I set and execute an ambitious agenda, putting the American people first."

Kushner did not take a salary for his position in the White House. Some of Kushner's early official duties included various government functions, working on Middle East policy decisions, and international trade deals.

To avoid conflicts of interest between his business decisions and decisions he would need to make in his new political appointment, Jared Kushner pledged to leave his job at Kushner Companies. Many questions were quickly raised after Trump appointed Kushner as a senior adviser. On January 9, 2017,

John Wagner and Ashley Parker, in the *Washington Post*, announced Kushner's appointment as a senior adviser. They stated:

> Some ethics experts question whether Kushner's appointment would violate the 1967 federal anti-nepotism law, which came about after President John F. Kennedy named his brother as attorney general. It forbids public officials from hiring family members in agencies or offices they oversee, and explicitly lists sons-in-law as prohibited employees.

White House ethics lawyers as well as the Justice Department examined the legality of Kushner's appointment and concluded that because the White House is not a government agency and because Kushner does not receive a salary, Trump's appointment of Kushner as a senior adviser does not violate ethics or nepotism laws.

CHAPTER 7

FROM THE BIG APPLE TO DC

From the start, Donald Trump's campaign and presidency was unconventional and controversial. As a result, leaving the private sector of business and real estate in New York City and transitioning to the public sector of politics in Washington, DC, was not without conflict for Ivanka Trump and Jared Kushner.

Since Donald Trump first took office, more than twenty people he appointed have either resigned or been fired. Secretary of State Rex Tillerson and FBI director James Comey were both fired by

On July 4, 2017, White House senior adviser Jared Kushner read a statement to reporters denying that he had had any improper involvement with the Russian government during Donald Trump's presidential campaign.

President Trump. Trump's press secretary Sean Spicer, chief strategist Steve Bannon, and White House communications director Hope Hicks all resigned over conflicts, controversy, and scandal. Despite the media's continued speculation that Trump's daughter and son-in-law would eventually leave Trump's administration, they have both remained. Both Trump and Kushner continue to be important fixtures in the Trump presidency.

IVANKA AND JARED IN POP CULTURE

Since joining the Trump campaign and then moving to Washington, Ivanka Trump and Jared Kushner have both appeared in popular culture media, political cartoons, comics, magazines, and TV spoofs. They have been a part of parody skits on *The Simpsons* and *Funny or Die* and have been portrayed several times in skits on *Saturday Night Live*. The popular late-night show has recurring skits starring Alec Baldwin as Donald Trump, and guest stars and cast members have parodied most of the Trump family. Actress Scarlett Johansson appeared as Ivanka Trump, for example, in one of the show's episodes.

Artists have also parodied Trump and Kushner as a power couple and members of the first family. *MAD Magazine* even featured the couple on its cover, along with President Trump. Popular political cartoon artist Hal Hefner has used Trump and Kushner as subjects for his Con$ume branded artwork. Hefner was known for creating pieces of pop art in 2015 based on the John Carpenter film *They Live*, where aliens are secretly living among humans on Earth. After the art became successful, Hefner went on to create the satirical art series called Con$ume.

RUSSIA INVESTIGATION AND SECURITY CLEARANCE

Before Donald Trump was sworn in as president, there was news that Russia had possibly interfered with the 2016 presidential election, as well as news that President Trump, or members of his campaign, may have been involved in this interference. The Justice Department set up a special investigation to look into the case.

The special counsel questioned Jared Kushner in November 2017 and again in April 2018, for a total of nine hours. On July 24, 2017, in the *New York Times*, Kushner gave a brief statement about the case to White House reporters, saying, "All of my actions were proper and occurred in the normal course of events of a very unique campaign … I did not collude with Russians, nor do I know of anyone in the campaign who did." As of December 2018, Ivanka Trump has not yet been questioned by the special counsel about the case.

As advisers to the president, both Trump and Kushner needed to be given security clearance so they could access sensitive information and could help advise the president on important decisions. Kushner was granted interim top-secret security clearance soon after being appointed into his official role as senior White House adviser. More than a year after the presidency began, both Trump and

G20 GERMANY 2017
HAMBURG

Kushner were given top-secret security clearance and given full authority in their roles as advisers.

Ivanka Trump (*third from left*) poses with world leaders in business, politics, and finance at the 2017 G20 Summit in Hamburg, Germany. She announced the Women Entrepreneurs Finance Initiative at the G20 Summit.

WE-FI: WOMEN ENTREPRENEURS FINANCE INITIATIVE

Before stepping into the world of politics, Ivanka Trump had written two books to help empower women in the world of business. In the early days of the Trump

ART COLLECTORS

As part of their personal family interests, Trump and Kushner support the arts by purchasing valuable art for their home. Some of the art can be seen on Trump's Instagram feed when she poses with her children. Works from contemporary American artists Nate Lowman, Dan Colen, and Christopher Wool and German artist David Ostrowski are part of their personal collection. In the *Guardian*, Nadja Sayej wrote that Trump has described the collection she started with Kushner as "a fun exploration of our personal and collective tastes." They started the collection after they married in 2009.

presidency, she continued as an advocate for women and became a strong supporter of female business owners in the United States and around the world. Several meetings and conversations, including one she had with Canadian prime minister Justin Trudeau and Jim Yong Kim, the president of the World Bank, led her to the idea of creating a global fund to help women around the world.

The global fund is called We-Fi, which stands for Women Entrepreneurs Finance Initiative. We-Fi is designed to provide small- and medium-sized businesses led by women access to financial products and services, mentors, and networking opportunities around the world. It is also meant to help governments

Ivanka and Kushner visit the Yad Vashem Holocaust Memorial Museum in Israel in 2017. President Trump and First Lady Melania Trump place a wreath in honor of the more than six million Jews killed by the Nazis during World War II.

improve environments for women in business.

We-Fi was announced at the G20 Summit in July 2017. The G20 Summit is an annual event in which members of the world's twenty leading economic countries gather to discuss future business and trade. By the time the 2017 G20 Summit took place, the We-Fi fund had accumulated $340 million from fourteen countries.

According to Carol E. Lee in the *Wall Street Journal*, Trump said, "As a female leader within the Trump administration, my focus is to help empower women in the United States and around the globe."

After helping to set up We-Fi, Trump has no formal involvement with the global funds or how they are used. However, she continues to publicly promote the fund and its ideals.

JERUSALEM EMBASSY

Before becoming president, Donald Trump pledged to recognize Jerusalem as the capital of Israel and to move the US embassy to Jerusalem from its original location in Tel Aviv, a heavily populated Israeli city. Trump also pledged to work with Israel to help achieve peace in the often conflict-plagued region. The controversies surrounding Israel go back to the nation's beginnings. Since Israel was first established by the United Nations after World War II, the land has been a part of growing conflicts between the Jewish people and Arab people who lived on the land, originally referred to as Palestine. Some Arab nations still do not recognize Israel as an independent nation, or Jerusalem as its capital.

From the beginning of Trump's presidency, Jared Kushner has worked on a peace proposal between Israel and the displaced Palestinian people in the region. Kushner also worked on President Trump's promise to have the US embassy in Israel moved to Jerusalem.

On December 6, 2017, President Trump delivered a speech from the Diplomatic Reception Room of the White House regarding his plans to formally recognize Jerusalem as the capital of

Israel and move the US embassy there. According to a *New York Times* transcript on December 6, 2017, President Trump said:

> Today we finally acknowledge the obvious. That Jerusalem is Israel's capital. This is nothing more or less than a recognition of reality. It is also the right thing to do ... That is why consistent with the Jerusalem embassy act, I am also directing the State Department to begin preparation to move the American embassy from Tel Aviv to Jerusalem. This will immediately begin the process ... so that a new embassy,

On May 13, 2018, Jared Kushner signs a guest book while visiting Israeli prime minister Benjamin Netanyahu (*right*) during the opening of the new US embassy in Jerusalem.

when completed, will be a magnificent tribute to peace.

On May 14, 2018, a temporary US embassy was opened in Jerusalem—the first for any country with embassies in Israel. Trump and Kushner were present to celebrate the event with other officials, including Israeli prime minister Benjamin Netanyahu. The embassy opening was largely symbolic, because construction on the site will take several years to complete. A recorded message from President Trump was presented at the event, and Ivanka Trump unveiled a dedication plaque and the seal of the US embassy during the ceremony.

> "When there is peace in this region, we will look back upon this day and remember that the journey to peace started with a strong America recognizing the truth."
> —JARED KUSHNER

According to Mark Moore in the *New York Post*, Ivanka Trump said, "On behalf of the 45th president of the United States of America, we welcome you officially and for the first time to the Embassy of the United States here in Jerusalem, the capital of Israel."

Jared Kushner also spoke during the event. According to Jeremy Diamond of CNN, Kushner said, "As Israel turns 70, the search for a lasting peace turns over a new leaf: one of realism and of not being afraid to stand strongly with our allies for what is good, for what is right, and for what is true … When there is peace in this region, we will look back upon this day and remember that the journey to peace started with a strong America recognizing the truth." Kushner also said, "While presidents before him backed down from their pledge to move the American embassy once in office, this President delivered. Because when President Trump makes a promise, he keeps it."

Trump's decision to move the US Embassy to Jerusalem is considered controversial, because some nations do not recognize Israel as a country or Jerusalem as its capital.

A POWER COUPLE'S FUTURE

As of October 2018, Trump and Kushner have proved critics in the media wrong with speculation that they would not last as advisers to President Trump. After they separated themselves from their previous financial ties, Trump and Kushner have both signaled that their time in Washington is something they are both serious about, at least while President Trump is in office.

Maggie Haberman and Katie Rogers, writing for the *New York Times*, quote Treasury secretary Steven Mnuchin as saying, "Any suggestion that they [Trump and Kushner] were going to leave the White House was just ridiculous ... They both have been dependable, valuable and effective partners for me and other members of the president's cabinet."

Both Trump and her husband have continued to work on projects that are close to their hearts and also help her father's presidency.

Trump held meetings both at her new Washington home as well as in the White House to help gain support for an expansion of the child tax credit to be included in President Trump's tax code reform. Trump also worked with Democrats and Republicans to have an expanded child tax credit included in tax cut legislation. The expanded child tax credit was included and the tax bill passed in 2017.

Kushner has had his own string of successes. While working with Mexico on trade, Kushner helped win a United States, Mexico, and Canada offer to jointly host the World Cup soccer championships in 2026. Following the news, Trump posted a picture on her Instagram account of Kushner holding a Kushner 26 USA jersey with the post, "Who is excited for the 2026 FIFA WorldCup??" followed by emojis of the American, Mexican, and Canadian flags.

On November 30, 2018, Kushner received more good news related to his trade negotiation work with the United States-Mexico-Canada Agreement (USMCA) at the G20 Summit in Buenos Aires, Argentina. Enrique Peña Nieto, Mexico's president, awarded Kushner Mexico's highest honor for foreigners—the Order of the Aztec Eagle—for his contributions in negotiating the USMCA. Two days later, Trump tweeted that she was thrilled about Jared's prestigous honor. Sarah Sanders, President Trump's press secretary, tweeted that the presentation of the award was an incredible moment for the whole Trump administration.

1981 Jared Corey Kushner is born on January 10 in Livingston, New Jersey, to Charles and Seryl Kushner. Ivana Marie Trump is born on October 30 in New York City to Donald and Ivana Trump.

2004 Ivanka Trump graduates summa cum laude from the Wharton School with a bachelor's degree in science of economics.

2006 Jared Kushner purchases the *New York Observer* for $10 million.

2007 Ivanka Trump and Jared Kushner meet at the Prime Grill steakhouse in Manhattan at a business lunch. Jared Kushner graduates from New York University with master's degrees in business and law. Ivanka Trump Fine Jewelry launches, as well as a new boutique on Madison Avenue bearing Ivanka's name.

2009 Ivanka Trump and Jared Kushner get married on October 25 at the Trump National Golf Club in Bedminster, New Jersey.

2011 Trump and Kushner's first child, Arabella Rose, is born on July 17.

2013 Trump and Kushner's second child, Joseph Frederick, is born on October 14.

2016 Trump and Kushner's third child, Theodore James, is born on March 27.

2017 Trump and Kushner begin serving as White House advisers to President Donald Trump. Trump's book *Women Who Work: Rewriting the Rules for Success* is released and profits from the sales are donated to charity. Trump's global fund initiative for female business owners, We-Fi, is announced at the G20 Summit.

2018 Trump and Kushner attend the opening of the US embassy in Jerusalem. Mexico's president awards Kushner with the Order of the Aztec Eagle, Mexico's highest honor for foreigners.

adviser A person who gives advice based on his or her expert experience in a given field.

collude To reach a secret understanding for a harmful purpose.

debt Money that is owed.

electoral college Appointed or chosen US citizens who cast formal votes for the presidential election.

embassy Office or residence of diplomats from a country, located in a foreign country.

entrepreneur A person who operates or organizes a business.

eponymous Bearing a personal name as a title.

ethics Moral correctness, or principles that guide a person's behavior.

G20 Summit An annual event in which members of the world's twenty leading economic countries gather to discuss future business and trade.

hedge fund Investors who use high-risk methods in hopes of large gains, such as investing borrowed money.

Holocaust Murder on a large scale, such as the systematic murder of more than six million Jews by the Nazis during World War II.

immigrate To come to live permanently in a country that is not one's own.

inauguration Formal beginning of an official's time in office.

interim In the meantime; temporary.

micro-targeting Marketing strategy that targets behavior to predict and influence future behavior.

nepotism The practice of hiring or favoring friends or relatives, such as hiring them for jobs.

parody A comical imitation of a literary or musical work.

philanthropy The act of giving or donating to groups or causes that need help, especially to help promote human welfare.

policy Ideas or principles that lead a government or business.

tax credit Amount of money deducted from what someone owes a government from its income or profits.

yin and yang In Chinese philosophy, two opposite concepts: yin is negative and feminine, yang is positive and masculine. The interaction of yin and yang is believed to preserve harmony and balance in the universe.

The Entrepreneurs' Organization (EO)
500 Montgomery Street, Suite 700
Alexandria, VA 22314
(703) 519-6700
Website: https://www.eonetwork.org
Facebook: @EntrepreneursOrganization
Twitter: @EntrepreneurOrg
The Entrepreneurs' Organization is a worldwide
    business network comprised of entrepreneurs from
    fifty-seven countries. The EO helps business owners
    achieve greater success by connecting them and
    enabling them to learn from one another.

Freechild Institute
PO Box 6185
Olympia, WA 98507-6185
(360) 489-9680
Website: https://freechild.org
Email: info@freechild.org
The Freechild Institute works to support young
    people through engagement, empowerment, and
    leadership.

Futurpreneur Canada
133 Richmond Street West, Suite 700
Toronto, ON M5H 2L3
Canada
(866) 646-2922
Website: https://www.futurpreneur.ca
Facebook: @futurpreneur
Twitter: @Futurpreneur
Futurpreneur Canada is a national, nonprofit
    organization that helps acquire financing and

training for young business owners, from ages
eighteen to thirty-nine.

Junior Achievement USA
One Education Way
Colorado Springs, CO 80906
(719) 540-8000
Website: https://www.juniorachievement.org/web
　/ja-usa/home
Facebook: @JuniorAchievementUSA
Twitter @JA_USA
Instagram: @juniorachievementusa
Junior Achievement USA is a youth-based organization
　that helps young people achieve success in the
　world economy.

Startup Canada
56 Sparks Street, Suite 300
Ottawa, ON K1P 5A9
Canada
Website: https://www.startupcan.ca
Facebook: @StartupCanada
Twitter: @Startup_Canada
Startup Canada is a group of Canadian entrepreneurs
　working together to help Canadian businesses'
　startup community.

Women Entrepreneurs Finance Initiative
Website: https://we-fi.org
Email: we-fi@worldbankgroup.org
We-Fi is a collaborative global partnership that seeks
　to provide financing for women-owned small
　businesses in developing countries.

Cuban, Mark, Shaan Patel, and Ian McCue. *Kid Start-Up: How YOU Can Become an Entrepreneur.* Las Vegas, NV: Diversion Books, 2017.

Doeden, Matt. *Ivanka Trump: A Brand of Her Own.* Minneapolis, MN: Lerner Publications Company, 2018.

Downs, Alison. *Cool Careers Without College for People Who Love Fashion* (Cool Careers Without College). New York, NY: Rosen Publishing, 2017.

Hinman, Bonnie. *Ivanka Trump: Businesswoman and Political Activist* (Newsmakers). Minneapolis, MN: ABDO Publishing, 2018.

Hoffman, Megan Mills. *Ivanka Trump: Entrepreneur and First Daughter.* New York, NY: Cavendish Square Publishing, 2018.

McKenna, James, Jeannine Glista, and Matt Fontaine. *How to Turn $100 into $1,000,000: Earn! Invest! Save!* New York, NY: Workman Publishing Company, 2016.

New York Times Editorial Staff. *Donald J. Trump* (Public Profiles). New York, NY: New York Times Educational Publishing, 2019.

Reid, Emily. *I Can Make Jewelry* (Makerspace Projects). New York, NY: Windmill Books, 2015.

Sedlackova, Jana. *The Complete Book of Fashion History: A Stylish Journey Through History and the Ultimate Guide for Being Fashionable in Every Era.* Lake Forest, CA: Walter Foster Jr., 2017.

Sullivan, George. *Scholastic Book of Presidents: A Book of U.S. Presidents.* New York, NY: Scholastic, 2016.

Wooten, Sara McIntosh. *Donald Trump: Real Estate Mogul and President* (Influential Lives). New York, NY: Enslow Publishing, 2017.

Apuzzo, Matt, and Maggie Haberman. " 'I Did Not
    Collude,' Kushner Says After Meeting Senate
    Investigators." *New York Times*, July 24, 2017.
    https://www.nytimes.com/2017/07/24/us
    /politics/jared-kushner-russia-senate.html.
Bar-Leib, Dov. "The Monumental Merit of Family
    Kushner." Israel Rising, January 23, 2017. https://
    www.israelrising.com/monumental-merit-kushner.
Berton, Brad. "Kushner Continues to Rebuild
    Empire, Buys 5,500 Units in August." *Multifamily
    Executive*, September 6, 2012. https://www
    .multifamilyexecutive.com/business-finance
    /business-trends/kushner-continues-to-rebuild
    -empire-buys-5-500-units-in-august_o.
Bertoni, Steven. "Exclusive Interview: How Jared
    Kushner Won Trump the White House." *Forbes*,
    November 22, 2016. https://www.forbes.com
    /sites/stevenbertoni/2016/11/22/exclusive
    -interview-how-jared-kushner-won-trump-the
    -white-house/#357629343af6.
Bertoni, Steven. "Josh Kushner's Complex World:
    How Jared's Liberal Brother Runs a Billion Dollar
    Fund in Trump Era." *Forbes*, April 25, 2017.
    https://www.forbes.com/sites/stevenbertoni
    /2017/04/10/josh-kushners-complicated-world
    -how-jareds-brother-runs-a-billion-dollar-fund
    -in-the-age-of-trump/#51b599a9f240.
Blair, Gwenda. *The Trumps: Three Generations
    That Built an Empire*. New York, NY: Simon &
    Schuster, 2001.
Bloom, Esther. "If You Think Trump's Money Comes
    from His Dad, You're Only Half Right." Billfold,

July 25, 2016. https://www.thebillfold
.com/2016/07/if-you-think-trumps-money
-comes-from-his-dad-youre-only-half-right.

Bondarenko, Veronika. "Jared Kushner Received a
Top New York Media Company as a $10 Million
'Graduation Present.' " Business Insider, June 1,
2017. https://www.businessinsider.com/jared
-kushner-received-the-observer-as-10-million
-graduation-present-2017-6.

Cohen, Rich. "How Jared Kushner Is Dismantling a
Family Empire." Vanity Fair, November 2017.
https://www.vanityfair.com/news/2017/09/jared
-kushner-family-empire-observer.

Cotliar, Sharon. "First Photo: 'Beautiful and Smart'
Ivanka Trump & Jared Kushner." People, October
26, 2009. https://people.com/celebrity/first
-photo-beautiful-and-smart-ivanka-trump-jared
-kushner.

Crum, Maddie. "How Did 'Power Couple' Become
the New Standard for Relationship Success?"
Huffington Post, July 18, 2016. https://www
.huffingtonpost.com/entry/power-couple-oed
_us_57893b84e4b03fc3ee50d7a0.

C-SPAN. "Donald Trump Presidential Campaign
Announcement." June 16, 2015. https://www
.c-span.org/video/?326473-1/donald-trump
-presidential-campaign-announcement.

Cummings, William, Fredreka Schouten, and John
Fritze. "Ivanka Trump, Jared Kushner Income
Tops at Least $81 Million Last Year." USA Today,
June 11, 2018. https://www.usatoday.com/story

/news/politics/2018/06/11/ivanka-trump
-jared-kushner-earn-more-than-81million
/693042002.

Dangremond, Sam. "How *Born Rich* Launched
Ivanka Trump and Burned Nearly Everyone Else."
Town & Country, May 10, 2017. https://www
.townandcountrymag.com/leisure/arts-and
-culture/a9044077/ivanka-trump-in-born-rich
-documentary.

Davidson, Joe. "Nepotism Aside, Kushner Is Part of
a Big Club When It Comes to Security Clearance
Problems." *Washington Post*, March 5, 2018.
https://www.washingtonpost.com/news
/powerpost/wp/2018/03/05/kushner-despite
-the-nepotism-welcome-to-the-club-of-security
-clearance-problems/?utm
-term=.7c41479e18ba.

Diamond, Jeremy. "Kushner's Split Screen Moment
in Jerusalem." CNN, May 14, 2018. https://
www.cnn.com/2018/05/14/politics/jared
-kushner-jerusalem-speech/index.html.

Dolsten, Josefin. "Supermodel Karlie Kloss Gets
Engaged to Joshua Kushner." *Times of Israel*, July
25, 2018. https://www.timesofisrael.com
/supermodel-karlie-kloss-gets-engaged-to
-joshua-kushner.

Edison Hayden, Michael. "Hillary Clinton Makes
History as Democratic Nominee." ABC News,
July 26, 2016. https://abcnews.go.com/Politics
/democrats-begin-convention-roll-call-amid
-divisions-ranks/story?id=40898573.

Elkies, Lauren. "Charles Kushner." *Real Deal*,
November 5, 2007. https://therealdeal.com
/closings/charles-kushner.

Features. "The Legacy." *New York*, Retrieved
September 3, 2018. http://nymag.com/news
/features/57891/index5.html.

Fox, Emily Jane. *Born Trump: Inside America's
First Family*. New York, NY: HarperCollins
Publishers, 2018.

Fox, Emily Jane. "The Strange, Complex Education
of Jared Kushner." *Vanity Fair*, December 5,
2016. https://www.vanityfair.com/news/2016
/12/jared-kushner-education-donald-trump.

Golden, Daniel. "How Did 'Less than Stellar' High
School Student Jared Kushner Get into Harvard?"
Guardian, November 18, 2016. https://www
.theguardian.com/commentisfree/2016/nov/18
/jared-kushner-harvard-donald-trump-son-in
-law.

Golden, Daniel. *The Price of Admission: How
America's Ruling Class Buys Its Way into Elite
Colleges—and Who Gets Left Outside the Gates*.
New York, NY: Crown, 2006.

Golden, Daniel. "The Story Behind Jared Kushner's
Curious Acceptance Into Harvard." ProPublica,
November 18, 2016. https://www.propublica
.org/article/the-story-behind-jared-kushners
-curious-acceptance-into-harvard.

Gossipmonger. "Oh, J-Vanka!" Intelligencer, *New
York*, May 4, 2007. http://nymag.com/daily
/intelligencer/2007/05/oh_jvanka.html.

Grant, Peter. "Kushner Family Closes Deal to Unload 666 Fifth Avenue." *Wall Street Journal*, August 3, 2018. https://www.wsj.com/articles/kushner -family-close-to-deal-to-unload-666-fifth -avenue-1533322813.

Gurley, George. "Trump Power: Ivanka Trump." *Marie Claire*, January 29, 2007. https://www .marieclaire.com/career-advice/tips/a105 /ivanka-trump.

Haberman, Maggie, and Rachel Abrams. "Ivanka Trump, Shifting Plans, Will Become a Federal Employee." *New York Times*, March 29, 2017. https://www.nytimes.com/2017/03/29/us /politics/ivanka-trump-federal-employee-white -house.html.

Haberman, Maggie, and Katie Rogers. "Still Standing, Jared Kushner and Ivanka Trump Step Back in the Spotlight." *New York Times*, July 28, 2018. https://www.nytimes.com/2018/07/28 /us/politics/jared-ivanka-trump.html.

Hamilton Blog. "Join Us As We Unveil the New Ivanka Trump Fine Jewelry Collection." Hamilton Jewelers, February 16, 2011. http://www .hamiltonjewelers.com/blog/2011/02/16 /join-us-as-we-unveil-the-new-ivanka-trump -fine-jewelry-collection.

Hand, Jafar. "Ivanka Trump's Book Seen as Boon for Afghan Women." VOA News, August 6, 2018. https://www.voanews.com/a/ivanka -trump-book-afghanistan-women/4515922 .html.

Henneberger, Melinda. "The Woman Trump Cherishes Most Is Daughter Ivanka." *Detroit News*, August 18, 2015. https://www .detroitnews.com/story/life/2015/08/18/woman -trump-cherishes-daughter-ivanka/31955397.

Hofstra University School of Law. "Hofstra Law Report." Winter 1997. https://law.hofstra.edu /pdf/alumni/hlr/hlr-1997-winter.pdf.

In Other News. "Jared Kushner and Ivanka Trump Sunder Relationship, Our Hearts." Intelligencer, *New York*, April 2, 2008. http://nymag.com /daily/intelligencer/2008/04/jared_kushner _and_ivanka_trump_2.html.

Ivankatrump. "Who Is Excited for the 2026 …" Instagram. https://www.instagram.com/p /BnCpZZgF_wj.

Johnson, Jamie, dir. *Born Rich*. 2003. Los Angeles, CA: Shout Factory, 2004. DVD.

Kranish, Michael. "Jared Kushner's Father on Probe into Family Company: 'We Are Not at All Concerned.' " *Washington Post*, January 22, 2018. https://www.washingtonpost.com /politics/jared-kushners-father-on-probe -into-family-company-we-are-not-at-all -concerned/2018/01/21/d8d39f9a-fabc-11e7 -a46b-a3614530bd87_story.html?utm_term =.de42ad4f7fdf.

La Ferla, Ruth. "Introducing the Ivanka." *New York Times*, December 27, 2007. https://www .nytimes.com/2007/12/27/fashion/27IVANKA .html?mtrref=undefined.

Lee, Carol E. "Saudi Arabia, U.A.E. Pledge $100 Million to World Bank's Women Entrepreneurs Fund." *Wall Street Journal*, May 21, 2017. https://www.wsj.com/articles/saudi-arabia-u-a -e-pledge-100-million-to-world-banks-women -entrepreneurs-fund-1495339028.

Liphshiz, Cnaan. "Jared Kushner's Family Is a Legend in this Belarus Town." *Times of Israel*, June 10, 2017. https://www.timesofisrael.com /jared-kushners-family-is-a-legend-in-this -belarus-town.

Lipsky-Karasz, Elisa. "Ivanka Trump: The Interview." *Harper's Bazaar*, May 16, 2011. https://www .harpersbazaar.com/celebrity/latest/news/a725 /ivanka-trump-interview.

Lowrey, Annie. "The Ivanka Fund." *Atlantic*, May 9, 2018. https://www.theatlantic.com/ideas /archive/2018/05/the-ivanka-fund/559949.

Mahler, Jonathan. "In Campaign and Company, Ivanka Trump Has a Central Role." *New York Times*, April 16, 2016. https://www.nytimes .com/2016/04/17/us/politics/ivanka-trump -donald-trump.html.

McAfee, Tierney. "Donald Trump Announces 2016 Bid: 'I'm Really Rich'—and That's Why I'm Running for President." *People*, June 16, 2015. https://people.com/celebrity/donald-trump-is -running-for-president-in-2016.

Michallon, Clemence, and Erica Tempesta. "The In-Laws Are in Town! Ivanka Trump and Jared Kushner Get a Visit from His Mom Seryl and

Convicted Criminal Dad Charles, as Their Cars Are Seen Being Loaded with Bags for a Weekend Away." *Daily Mail*, December 15, 2017. https://www.dailymail.co.uk/femail/article-5184507/Jared-Kushners-parents-spotted-D-C-home.html.

Moore, Mark. "US Embassy Officially Opens in Jerusalem." *New York Post*, May 14, 2018. https://nypost.com/2018/05/14/us-embassy-officially-opens-in-jerusalem.

New York Times. "Full Video and Transcript: Trump's Speech Recognizing Jerusalem as the Capital of Israel." December 6, 2017. https://www.nytimes.com/2017/12/06/world/middleeast/trump-israel-speech-transcript.html.

Observer staff. "666 Fifth Avenue Deal Closes." Observer, January 30, 2007. https://observer.com/2007/01/666-fifth-avenue-deal-closes.

Oxford University Press. "Power Couple." English Oxford Living Dictionaries. Retrieved October 3, 2018. https://en.oxforddictionaries.com/definition/power_couple.

PageSix.com staff. "Ivanka Observed." Page Six, *New York Post*, April 20, 2007. https://pagesix.com/2007/04/20/ivanka-observed/?_ga=1.18346993.939471382.1471614553.

PageSix.com staff. "Unattached." Page Six, *New York Post*, April 2, 2008. https://pagesix.com/2008/04/02/unattached/?_ga=2.73032657.354308040.1535406305-186374853.1528549418.

Party Lines. "Jared Kushner and Ivanka Trump Are Just Friends. Really." Intelligencer, *New York*, April 19, 2007. http://nymag.com/daily /intelligencer/2007/04/jared_kushner_and _ivanka_trump.html.

Party Lines. "On the Hunt for J-Vanka at the Whitney Party: Success!" Intelligencer, *New York*, June 7, 2007. http://nymag.com/daily/intelligencer /2007/06/on_the_hunt_for_jvanka_at_the.html.

Petrs, Jeremy W. "Citizen Kushner." *New York Times*, June 24, 2011. https://www.nytimes .com/2011/06/26/fashion/life-in-the-fishbowl -for-jared-kushner.html.

Piore, Adam. "Behind the Record Deal for 666 Fifth Avenue." *Real Deal*, October 22, 2007. https:// therealdeal.com/issues_articles/behind -the-record-deal-for-666-fifth-avenue.

Philanthropy News Digest. "Trump Gives $1 Million Matching Grant to United Way of New York City." February 12, 2003. https:// philanthropynewsdigest.org/news/trump-gives-1 -million-matching-grant-to-united-way-of-new -york-city.

Reuters. "What Is Jared Kushner's Role In Donald Trump's Campaign?" *Newsweek*, April 4, 2016. https://www.newsweek.com/jared-kushner -ivanka-trump-donald-trump-real-estate-2016 -presidential-election-443987.

Rice, Andrew. "The Young Trump." Intelligencer. *New York*, January 9, 2017. http://nymag.com/daily

/intelligencer/2017/01/jared-kushner-trump
-administration-power.html.

Salkin, Allen. "The Education of a Publisher." *New York Times*, March 11, 2007. https://www
.nytimes.com/2007/03/11/fashion/11jared.

Sayej, Nadja. "What's Inside Ivanka Trump's Male -Dominated $25m Art Collection?" *Guardian*, July 27, 2017. https://www.theguardian.com /artanddesign/2017/jul/27/ivanka-trump-jared -kushner-art-collection.

Scott, Eugene. "Trump Ally: Ivanka Trump's New Gig Isn't Nepotism Because She Isn't Being Paid." CNN, March 30, 2017. https://www.cnn .com/2017/03/30/politics/ivanka-trump-jason -miller-nepotism-cnntv/index.html.

Segers, Grace. "Jared Kushner Receives 'Aztec Eagle' award from the Mexican Government." CBS News, November 30, 2018. https://www .cbsnews.com/news/jared-kushner-receives -aztec-eagle-award-from-mexican-government.

Shelbourne, Mallory. "Jared Kushner Named Senior Adviser to Trump." Hill, January 9, 2017. https:// thehill.com/homenews/administration /313268-kushner-to-be-named-senior-adviser -to-trump-report.

Sherman, Gabriel. "Ivanka Trump on New Fiancé Jared Kushner: 'He'll Be a Great Father.' " Intelligencer, *New York*, July 17, 2009. http:// nymag.com/daily/intelligencer/2009/07/ivanka _trump_on_new_fiance_jar.html.

Sherman, Gabriel. "The Legacy." *New York*, July 12, 2009. http://nymag.com/news/features /57891/#print.

Smothers, Ronald. "Democratic Donor Receives a Two-Year Prison Sentence." *New York Times*, March 5, 2005. https://www.nytimes .com/2005/03/05/nyregion/democratic-donor -receives-twoyear-prison-sentence.html.

Solomon, Daniel. "Meet Nicole Kushner, Jared's Visa-Hawking Sister." Fast Forward, May 10, 2017. https://forward.com/fast-forward /371513/meet-nicole-kushner-jareds-visa -hawking-sister.

Spiers, Elizabeth. "No, Jared Kushner, It Was Not Okay to Delete My Journalists' Work." *Washington Post*, August 9, 2018. https://www .washingtonpost.com/news/posteverything /wp/2018/08/09/no-jared-kushner-it-wasnt -okay-to-delete-my-journalists-work /?noredirect=on&utm_term=.aa7759c7f740.

Steinhauer, Jennifer. "Her Cheekbones (High) or Her Name (Trump)." *New York Times*, August 17, 1997. https://www.nytimes.com/1997/08/17 /style/her-cheekbones-high-or-her-name-trump .html.

Strauss, Valerie. "Trump's Influential Son-in-Law Went to Harvard. Is This How Jared Kushner Got In?" *Washington Post*, November 19, 2016. https://www.washingtonpost.com/news/answer -sheet/wp/2016/11/19/trumps-influential-son-in

-law-went-to-harvard-is-this-how-jared-kushner
-got-in/?utm_term=.ad9c416e8c30.

Trump, Ivana. *Raising Trump*. New York, NY: Gallery
Books, 2017.

Trump, Ivanka. *The Trump Card: Playing to Win in
Work and Life*. New York, NY: Touchstone, 2010.

Trump, Ivanka. "When My Father Takes Office …"
Facebook, January 11, 2017. https://www
.facebook.com/IvankaTrump/posts/when-my
-father-takes-office-as-the-45th-president-of-the
-united-states-of-americ/10154998180397682.

United States Holocaust Memorial Museum. "Rae
Kushner." Retrieved September 2, 2018. https://
encyclopedia.ushmm.org/content/en/article/rae
-kushner.

Vadnal, Julie. "Trump This: Ivanka's New Business
Memoir." *Elle*, October 16, 2009. https://www
.elle.com/culture/books/reviews/a10569/trump
-this-ivankas-new-business-memoir-382960.

Van Meter, Jonathan. "Ivanka Trump Knows What
It Means to Be a Modern Millennial." *Vogue*,
February 25, 2015. https://www.vogue.com
/article/ivanka-trump-collection-the-apprentice
-family.

Vick, Karl. "Family First: The Trials of Jared Kushner."
Time, June 1, 2017. http://time.com/4800796
/the-trials-of-jared-kushner.

Wagner, John, and Ashley Parker. "Trump's Son-
in-law, Jared Kushner, to Join White House
as Senior Adviser; No Formal Role for Ivanka
Trump." *Washington Post*, January 9, 2017.

https://www.washingtonpost.com/news/post
-politics/wp/2017/01/09/tumps-son-in-law
-jared-kushner-expected-to-join-white-house-as
-a-senior-adviser/?utm_term=.069a7b32d14a.

Weiss, Lois. "Kushner Sells $525M Stake." *New York Post*, April 26, 2008. https://nypost.com
/2008/04/26/kushner-sells-525m-stake.

Widdicombe, Lizzie. "Ivanka and Jared's Power Play." *New Yorker*, August 22, 2016. https://
www.newyorker.com/magazine/2016/08/22
/ivanka-trump-and-jared-kushners-power
-play?mbid=synd_digg.

Zurcher, Anthony. "What's the Deal with the Trump Foundation?" BBC, October 4, 2016. https://
www.bbc.com/news/election-us-2016
-37369515.

C

children, of Trump and Kushner, 51, 53, 55, 67
Choate Rosemary Hall, 17, 18, 19
Clinton, Hillary, 26–27, 59, 62, 63, 64, 65

D

dating, 8, 31, 35–36, 38
Dynamic Diamond Corpfish, 20, 44

F

first meeting, 8, 35
Frisch School, 21, 29

G

G20 Summit, 81–82, 87

H

Harvard University, 6, 21, 28, 29, 30
Holocaust, 22–23, 24, 25

I

Instagram, 28, 54
Ivanka Trump lifestyle brand, 6, 20, 22, 44, 45

fashion, 20, 22, 45
Ivanka Trump Fine Jewelry, 9, 20, 39, 44, 45, 69

J

"Javanka," 6, 36, 71
Jerusalem, 83, 84, 85, 86

K

Kushner, Arabella Rose, 53, 55, 67
Kushner, Charles, 6, 22, 23, 24, 26, 30, 32
Hebrew name, 22–23
parents, 22–23, 24
politics, 26–27
prison time, 30–31, 32, 47
Kushner, Jared, 6, 21, 22, 27, 29–30, 31, 32, 33, 35, 36, 38, 39, 40, 41, 42, 43, 46, 47, 48, 49, 50, 51, 53–54, 55, 58, 60, 61, 62–63, 64, 67–68, 70, 71, 72, 73–75, 76, 77, 78, 79, 81, 83, 85–86, 87
campaign efforts, 58, 60, 61, 62–63, 64

degrees, 6, 21, 31, 32
early life, 21, 22
education, 6, 8, 21,
    29–30, 31, 32
newspaper owner, 8,
    28, 31, 35
parents, 6, 22–23
philanthropist, 46
political leanings,
    26–27, 58, 60
presidential adviser, 8,
    68, 70, 73–74, 79,
    83, 86
private personality, 43,
    49, 53–54
real estate career, 30,
    35, 47, 48, 54
religion, 21, 22, 36,
    38, 40
siblings, 27–28
trade negotiator, 87
target marketing, 63
unpaid adviser, 74
Kushner, Joseph, 24,
    25–26, 27
Kushner, Joseph
    Frederick, 55, 67
Kushner, Joshua, 28–29
Thrive Capital, 27
Kushner, Rae, 22–23,
    25–26
Kushner, Theodore
    James, 55, 59, 67

Kushner Companies,
    27, 28, 30, 35, 47,
    48, 54, 75

M

marriage, 6, 8, 43, 51
Modern Orthodox
    Judaism, 21, 22, 36,
    38, 40
Sabbath, 40–41, 53

N

nepotism, 72, 75
New York Observer, 8,
    28, 31, 54
editor, 31, 54
online only, 31, 54
New York University
    (NYU), 21, 23, 28,
    31, 32

P

philanthropy, 46
Donald J. Trump
    Foundation, 46
Ivanka M. Trump
    Foundation, 73
political players, 76–77
Bannon, Steve, 77
Hicks, Hope, 61, 77
Mnuchin, Steven, 86
Sanders, Sarah, 87
Sessions, Jeff, 61

Spicer, Sean, 77
Tillerson, Rex, 76
pop culture, 78
  parodied, 78
  TV appearances,
    53–54
power couples, 6
  definition of, 8
  examples, 8, 71

S

666 Fifth Avenue, 47,
  48, 49, 54

T

Trump, Barron William,
  17, 41
Trump, Donald J., 6, 8,
  9, 10, 17, 31, 51,
  56, 58, 63, 83
Art of the Deal, The, 46
businessman, 9, 56
campaign for
  presidency, 57, 59–
  60, 63, 76
education, 10
marrriages, 9, 12, 17
president of the
  United States, 6, 8,
  9, 10, 55, 56, 64,
  65–66, 69, 76, 83,
  84–85, 86
real estate tycoon, 9

reality television star, 9
Trump, Donald John Jr.,
  12, 14, 15, 67
Trump, Eric Frederick,
  13, 14, 15, 67
Trump, Frederick, 10,
  13–14
Trump, Ivana, 6, 11–
  12, 18
competitive skier, 11
education, 11–12
modeling career, 6,
  12, 18
Raising Trump, 16
Trump, Ivanka, 6, 8,
  9, 10, 13, 14, 15,
  16–19, 33, 35, 36,
  38, 39, 40, 41, 42,
  43, 44, 45, 46, 49,
  50, 51, 52, 53–54,
  55, 56, 58, 59–60,
  67–68, 69, 70, 71,
  72, 73, 76, 77, 78,
  79, 80–81, 82–83,
  85, 89
author, 6, 9, 51–52,
  72–73, 80
ballet, 16
birth, 13
business owner, 6, 9,
  20, 33, 44, 45
campaign
  spokesperson, 58,
  59–60

child tax credit, 87
conversion to Modern
  Orthodox Judaism,
  38, 39, 40, 41
early life, 13, 14, 15, 16
education, 10, 16–18
film and TV personality,
  9, 51
Instagram account, 50,
  81, 87
legal name, 13
modeling career, 6, 9,
  18–20
mother, 43, 51, 53, 55
parents, 6, 10, 11–12
philanthropist, 46, 73
presidential adviser, 8,
  10, 67–68, 69, 70,
  71, 79, 86
public life, 49–50
real estate developer,
  9, 14
security clearance, 79
siblings, 12, 13
*Trump Card: Playing to
  Win in Work and Life,
  The*, 51–52
Twitter account, 39, 42,
  50, 53, 55, 87
unpaid adviser, 72

use of social media, 49,
  53, 55, 69, 73, 87
vice president in the
  Trump Organization,
  6, 20, 33, 44, 51, 69
*Women Who Work:
  Rewriting the Rules for
  Success*, 72–73
Trump, Tiffany Ariana,
  17, 41
Trump Organization, 6,
  13–14, 20, 44
  founding of, 14
Trump Tower, 6, 13, 14,
  35, 57, 58
Twitter, 50, 54

U

US embassy, 83, 84,
  85, 86

W

wedding, 39, 41, 46
  cake, 41–42
Wharton School of
  Business, 10, 18
Women Entrepreneurs
  Finance Initiative
  (We-Fi), 81, 82–83

ABOUT THE AUTHOR

Adam Furgang's writing credits include numerous nonfiction books in the middle school market. His works include biographies about Rick Riordan, Edward Snowden, and Jeff Bezos. Furgang has a background in art, design, and photography, and he lives in upstate New York with his wife and two sons.

PHOTO CREDITS

Cover Bloomberg/Getty Images; p. 7 Larry Busacca/Getty Images; p. 11 New York Daily News Archive/Getty Images; p. 12 Jack Mitchell/Archive Photos/Getty Images; pp. 15, 16 Ron Galella/Getty Images; p. 19 Richard Levine/Corbis News/Getty Images; pp. 23, 29, 37, 49 Patrick McMullan/Getty Images; p. 25 Viktor Drachev/TASS/Getty Images; p. 32 Chris Hondros/Getty Images; p. 34 Peter Kramer/Getty Images; p. 42 Handout/Getty Images; p. 44 Everett Collection Inc/Alamy Stock Photo; pp. 45, 80 © AP Photo; p. 52 Mathew Imaging/FilmMagic/Getty Images; p. 57 Christopher Gregory/Getty Images; p. 61 Rick Friedman/Corbis News/Getty Images; p. 62 Mark Wilson/Getty Images; p. 66 Pool/Getty Images; p. 68 Jim Watson/AFP/Getty Images; p. 72 Anadolu Agency/Getty Images; p. 74 picture alliance/Getty Images; p. 77 Xinhua News Agency/Getty Images; p. 82 Gali Tibbon/AFP/Getty Images; p. 84 US State Department/Alamy Stock Photo; additional interior pages design elements Levchenko Ilia/Shutterstock.com (light streaks), Shmizla/Shutterstock.com (dot pattern), Romeo Budai/EyeEm/Getty Images (sparkle backgrounds).

Design and Layout: Nicole Russo-Duca; Senior Editor: Kathy Kuhtz Campbell; Photo Researcher: Sherri Jackson